# THE STAIRWAY TO FREEDOM

## A MESSAGE FROM THE GREAT WHITE BROTHERHOOD

**Bob Sanders**

# DISCLAIMERS

# COPYRIGHT

This book was authored by Bob Sanders and messaged to him from The Great White Brotherhood by clairaudience, or as some people call "channelling". It is for everyone to read for spiritual advancement.

Please tell everyone about this book to help spread the messages it contains.

For more information please visit the following internet sites:

https://www.thestairwaytofreedom.org

https://www.youtube.com/channel/UC2UDv0r4mtNPEWbve5YHDeg/

https://plus.google.com/117982922208354739833

First edition - March 2016

# PREFACE

This book "Stairway To Freedom" was dictated to me by clairaudience, or as some people call channelling, by a group of beings that call themselves The Great White Brotherhood. It is a guide to you and for you for your spiritual advancement.

## Who is The Great White Brotherhood?

The Great White Brotherhood is a group of people who claim to have lived an incarnation here on Earth, have since passed on to what is sometimes called Heaven, or the spirit realms, and have decided to come back close to Earth to pass on their knowledge to us who are incarnate at the moment. They, the brotherhood, are at various levels of spiritual advancement, some far removed from the low vibrations that we experience on Earth, others not so advanced. They join their thoughts together in a chain, passing information from one to another, from highest to lowest, until, finally, the information is implanted into the mind of someone on the Earth plane who has been trained to receive such information.

In this case, it was I. I must stress, at this point, that I have no special qualifications to be part of the brotherhood except that I was chosen by them many years ago among many others, no doubt, to permit them to work on Earth because, as they are spirit and have no physical bodies, they cannot directly communicate with the majority of the population incarnate on Earth. Thus, I was trained to become clairaudient, which is quite simply the ability to receive information in my mind sent from the mind of someone else. This enables a message or information to be sent from them through me to the person for whom the message is intended.

In principle, it is quite simple. I try to clear my mind of any thoughts coming from me, open a channel to them, who do the same, and the information flows. I hear the information as if I was talking to myself in my head except that I have no idea, in advance, of the contents of the information being transmitted. I try to capture the thoughts as clearly as I can and pass them on as required.

**Warning:** I would strongly advise anyone who wishes to develop the gifts of the spirit, as they are called, not to do so without the help of competent and qualified teachers as it can be extremely dangerous. The reason is that if one opens one's mind into the astral realms, one is almost sure to attract the attention of a force in the low astral realm that would be of evil intent. The result could be catastrophic for that person. The low astral plane is full of horrible thought forms plus creatures designed by nature to live there and also the dregs of humanity who have died and are stuck in that plane. Unfortunately, to reach the true spiritual realms, one has first to pass through that low astral plane. With protection, one can achieve this. Without protection, one would be exposed to any and all of these horrible manifestations. You would not wish to be a victim of these forces.

So, I repeat, do not try to develop the gifts without proper training and protection. The technique for attracting teachers and for developing the gifts is fully described in the book so I will not repeat it here.

**Other spiritual beings.**

At the time when this book was being transmitted to me in the 1980s, internet did not exist as far as the public was concerned and so, although everybody had heard of visitors from space, etcetera, very little information about them was available. The White Brotherhood flatly refused to talk to me about them and so it is only recently that I have found out that there are apparently groups of people from other planets, star systems, or dimensions that are here to help us in a similar manner to that of the brotherhood. Whether the intent of these people is truly spiritual, I cannot say. Whether they coordinate their efforts with the brotherhood, I do not know. Certainly, the message is very similar but we should sift the information given with caution, accepting only that which rings true in our hearts and rejecting that which seems doubtful.

**Why publish now?**

This book, "The Stairway To Freedom", was dictated to me over a period of months, starting in 1980. I was asked to make it freely available to the public so I tried to have it published at that time without success. So I shelved the idea, waiting until an alternative means of presenting information to everybody became available. The time is now ripe. The information contained in this book is as valid now as when it was presented to me and, thanks to the internet, it can be presented to you for free all over the world.

I have recently been pushed by the brotherhood to take the necessary steps to give you this information. You may make of it what you will. From experience, I know that you will react in one of three ways. Some will read the first page or two and turn to other more appealing activities. Others will be scandalised and do all in their power to deny the validity of the information. The third group will find that the book quite simply changes their lives.

To those in the first group, I say, be patient. One day, you will be ready for this. To those in the second group, I say that I understand. For information to be accepted by the mind, pigeonholes have to be made for that information to be placed within. If you do not yet have a pigeonhole made for that type of information, you have no choice but to reject such information. Do not blame yourself. It is perfectly natural. One day, perhaps you too will be able to accept the truth presented to you in this publication. To the last group, I say, welcome. Join with us if you wish. Join the brotherhood and by following the precepts presented in the book, follow the advice peacefully and calmly and with patience. You do not have to play an active role if you are not ready. By the simple act of prayer, meditation, and service to your fellow man, you will be acting in harmony with the brotherhood and helping to reduce the hatred and violence in the world.

# PRAYERS

Now, before you start reading the book, I would like you to read two prayers that I was given by a person who presented himself to me as **Father Ignatius**. These two prayers were given to me in 1985 and are as follows.

The first prayer is called:

**Blessed Is The Name Of The Lord**.

"Blessed is the name of the Lord. Blessed is His city and blessed those who would aspire to reach it. Come with me and we shall walk together. Together we shall traverse desert and swamp. Together we shall arrive at sanctuary and together shall our feet be bathed. Such is our destiny. The road is infinite, the goal always in sight. Nothing will prevent the path from taking us there. So we travel in peace, enjoying each and every moment. We bless the path and God blesses us. We bless the difficulties and we are blessed. Blessed is the name of the Lord."

Now the second one is more of a poem, really, describing the way that people in the spiritual world view the situation with regard to us and it's called:

**The Way Forward And The Way Back**.

"Once there was a time, oh so long ago, that those whose minds reach back to it are scarcely here, and though, through devious routes and channels, mankind likes to live, we trust that, in the long and short-term, he also learns to give. Can it be that pain and sorrow are always ever-near and can it be that happiness is often tinged with fear? Or too often we find, as we pass the veil, that beauty, love, and understanding were there. To no avail it is that we look back with sorrow. We should have learned to live our lives in God and not in mammon. Tomorrow, always sought and never to be found, was always beckoning us, and still we found that life was full of tears. We worked, we cursed, we tried, and yes, we failed to put ourselves in order that we might have rent the veil between this life and the next, between a life of happiness and a time spent perplexed and wondering still if there was any point in going on. At last, one day, we found to our dismay that we had somehow passed beyond the veil and still we look with sorrow at the work that was unspent on things to do with God and not a life of discontent. Therefore, we vowed we would return to the life that we had spent on Earth and, into that life, we would put an everlasting supplement to others to seek God foremost and mammon not at all. Then perhaps we too could rest within the marbled hall of peace and tranquility. Ensure that you who read these words and find them to be true that you put them into practice and join with us in peace and love within the marbled hall."

# FOREWORD

Should those who are troubled in their hearts and minds concerning the validity of experience gained during meditation and prayer seek reassurance that those experiences are valid, cogent, and based upon reality there are, unfortunately, no books, manuals, or primers to which he can refer for verification. This is because his experiences in the astral realms make use of the same faculties that the imagination also use and, therefore, any experiences noted by those who, by nature or by intent, are able to enter the astral realms tend to be ignored or put aside, expecting them to be a figment of that imagination and, therefore, to have no basis in reality.

Traditionally, those people who have the strength of personality enabling them to command the attention of the public through speeches and publications and who might have been able to explain to the public that psychic experiences can be valid had been barred from doing so by that very strength of personality, that level headedness so admired by those of the Earth.

The few prophets and soothsayers that have existed throughout the long ages of man have been generally dismissed by establishment as being of unsound mind. The result, as was mentioned above, is that explorers into the realms of spirituality are forced, by and large, to travel alone and forge experience for themselves, testing its validity by the old adages composed to test the value of experience. This unsatisfactory state of affairs has existed for far too long and it has been decreed that it should no longer continue to be.

There is a movement afoot to present to the world sufficient information written in plain language that will enable all students of the mysteries of life to use as handbooks for their journeys. There is no danger of abuse of this information by those of evil intent. Spirituality, is gaining and its use, is a function of soul growth and that can only be gained by those following the path towards God. All others are standing still in terms of soul growth or are actually going backwards if they are involved in harmful activities.

So the information to be revealed would be of no use to such people. They may wish to experiment but would be unable to operate in the spiritual realms. Just as a man may leap from a cliff-top to test his abilities to fly like a bird, without the correct equipment, he merely plunges to destruction on the rocks below. Similarly, the uninitiated would be barred from entering the larger realities of life until he had equipped himself through prayer, meditation, and devotion to God for so doing.

It is intended that the information released through instruments chosen for their suitability will form the basis of every individual spirit growth, not only whilst incarnate on Earth, but will continue into the life hereafter, that such information will be correlated into a cohesive set that will, in essence, interrelate with similar information being transmitted throughout the world. Thus, we wish to present that the information will be at one with all truth that has or will be presented to the public.

It is in the interest of the student to sift such information as he comes across to ensure that it touches his soul with truth and to reject that which is clearly the figment of the imagination of someone who, without having achieved the necessary soul growth so as to have acquired universal wisdom, nevertheless has produced information purporting to be of spiritual value. With a little practice and some spiritual development, the student will quickly sift the wheat from the chaff.

We look forward to the day when library shelves and the homes of peace-loving peoples throughout the world are equipped with the necessary information so as to allow the young from a very early age, when purity is automatic and soul growth could be more easily achieved, to have access to the relevant information to set them upon the path that religions throughout time have tried to do and have failed. We look forward to the day when, as the truth concerning the oneness of all mankind is realised, that the peoples of the world lay down their weapons, refuse to fight, open the barriers between countries, and celebrate the God made manifest in man. Such a day, whilst far off at the moment, is destined to occur and it behoves all who can to speed that day.

Further, it is anticipated that the day will dawn when man incarnate on Earth and man discarnate in spirit will communicate freely as was intended. Then, truly, will all barriers have been lowered and the beauty of God's creation will shine in the glory that has for so long been prevented by the tarnish of ego and hate complexes. Do not be put off or dismayed by the apparent length of the journey. Do not take account of the warnings and admonitions of those who would view such freedom with horror and fear. Do not be convinced that religion is more important than the development of the power of God within you as an individual nor yet be persuaded that you have to bow down to any man, any force, any deity, other than God.

Should you have already achieved the necessary development, you will understand the meaning of these words. You will have already doubted the value of patriotism, of religious dogma, of conventionality and conformity to a norm created by those tied to the Earth and whose souls sleep still. Prepare to leave those people sleeping still and take the path to freedom. The way is ready, the path made smooth, and the goal awaits you. Join us, brother and sister, and be welcome as one with us and with God.

Such is the destiny of man. How sad that through fear, ignorance, and for the sake of power, religious leaders, politicians, and leaders of trades unions, etcetera, have chained their fellow man to the shackles of their own ideas. This state of affairs is doomed to failure and must end. The time, as always, is ever-ripe. The message contained within these lines was given by the Master Jesus many years ago and was stated by the various prophets before and after, and still, the world is in chains, both physical and metaphoric. This is an abomination to the concept of God. It is up to all individuals, when ready, to take the path alone to God.  Others they will meet en route and, finally, they will join the mass of liberated souls constantly celebrating the beauty and wonder of life.

Stay no longer in the shadows of the fear portrayed by those who know no better. Step into the light and join the pilgrims, the prophets, and the master on the road to perfection. You will never regret it and you will never again be swayed into areas of hate by those who have used and abused you for their own doubtful ends. They will have no further hold on you. You will be beyond their grasp and the power of God, his angelic forces, will protect you from them.

The anguish of the fallen ones will be great initially as they see their flock disappearing into the arms of God one by one. They will use all the forces at their disposal to prevent it from happening, but, remember, the power of God is greater than the power of evil. The power of God is further strengthened by every soul who turns to God and does God's work. The power of evil is diminished in the same respect. Ultimately, the good will triumph and wars, strife, and unhappiness will cease.

# CHAPTER 1 - THE POWER OF GOD

.

Let us consider the source of God's power - that substance which has been called the breath of life, odic force, and which may simply be termed the power of God. We know from observation of all that we can see that some force is used to control the growth and character of all things. The plants of Earth grow from seed to maturity at certain seasons of the year in such a bewildering and splendid variety of shapes, colours, and perfumes that it seems almost impossible that any single intelligence could have created them. The animals of the Earth and seas abound in unceasing variety. The planets of our universe are permitted to wander through the Heavens, seen as myriad points of light but are held in an invisible grip.

Behind the haphazard plethora of shapes, we detect a controlling force. The plants are reborn each year, responding to an invisible, silent call. They are reborn true in their species. The rose does not combine with the dandelion nor lavender with the hop. Without being controlled in any way that we can detect, the plants have a means of knowing which other plants are suitable partners for cross-fertilisation. Similarly, animals follow guidelines set out for their development and regeneration. The lion does not mate with the lamb nor the horse with the pig. Each animal, according to his species, senses the time of year for performing certain acts like breeding, migrating, or hibernating. The creatures obey these commands quite unconsciously because the call, the power, is irresistible.

It is our task now to consider this force and to try and understand how complex and yet how simple is the nature of God's power. By understanding a little more, it may be possible for us to take one step nearer God's throne. When God created the physical universe, all that our earthly senses can relate to, he created it of atoms, structures so tiny that man has only recently developed machines to observe and quantify them. Each atom is a miniature form of planet. By observing atoms moving round each other in an endlessly repeated pattern to form an object that we may observe with our naked eyes, we think perhaps that our universe appears like that to some other being too gigantic for us to sense. Everything that exists in the universe is composed of atoms combining in various ways to make the structures that we see and sense. Our physical bodies, the plants, rocks, air, the seas, our thoughts and emotions – everything is composed of atoms combining in some way.

Each atom has a power inside it, the power of God. That power is not only contained inside the atom but extends for a distance beyond. This radiating force is called magnetism by scientists. Atoms, therefore, attract each other according to the nature of the power exuding from that atom. Atoms may combine into quite complicated structures and produce substances such as sugars and plastics. Man on Earth has obtained some idea of the power contained in each atom because he has recently learned to unleash that power. It was not God's intention that the power should be released in such a fashion. It will be shown in this chapter that the power can be released, contained, and put to use in a safe manner by an act of spiritual will according to God's law.

Scientists have stumbled on a means of releasing this power in a crude fashion and there is great danger because the people who have control of it may not be spiritually advanced enough to put the power to use in God's name. There are always destructive, base powers lurking, ready to influence the minds of man in many subtle ways. The spiritually immature person would be impressed by arguments presented in a way that would appeal to his low ego. The result has already been seen in various parts of the world - the wanton destruction of physical lives, the disfiguration and corruption of human form and desecration of land. The power of God is not to be used in such a fashion. His people, His animals, plants, kingdoms are not to be destroyed because of the base instincts and fears of any group of individuals. The price in remorse eventually to be paid by these misguided souls will greatly outweigh the suffering that they have brought to their victims. They will ultimately learn, as must we all, that respect for God's kingdom is of paramount importance. Preservation of self means nothing compared to this.

The power of God, when put to use in God's name to further his work, is regenerated. As this power is used, so more is sent down to us for further use. Only when it is used for destructive purposes is the supply cut off and then, to continue such work, it is necessary to draw on the vital forces of one's own body. Students of the black arts and those who actively plot evil against others would do well to take heed of this. God's power belongs to him. It is to be used for good work. He gives us free will to act as we please but he reserves the right to control that power and issue it only to those who do his work. People doing evil work will find that in order to continue to project force against others, their vital force gradually diminishes until tiredness, sickness, feebleness of mind, disease, and death are experienced. A brief study of the history of mankind will reveal that, of all the people notorious through acts of evil against God, few indeed lived to attain old age and good health. Compare that with the data concerning the number of genuine disciples of God, priests, nuns, and ordinary good souls, who achieve longevity and vibrant health. God indeed looks after His own.

God is spirit and His power is spirit. Magnetism, gravity – call it what you will – is a spirit force. It is invisible to the physical eyes but may be observed spiritually as light, the colour of which varies according to the use being made of it. In complex structures like man, the power is used in a variety of ways – maintaining physical life, permitting thoughts to be formulated in the brain, fighting diseases, aspiring to God, etcetera.

The essential foundation of life force is that which we call the power of God. The exact nature of the force may not be quantified. It is deemed to remain forever the ultimate mystery. Its effects are all around us, that which is seen and that which is unobservable. However, the motivating force itself is never observed. It may be that the power that motivates all life is observed in many and varied forms but that power itself has one source and is one power. It is not a part of the one power that motivates but the totality of power that is the essence of anything manifest.

To stress the point, the one singular life force is at the focus of everything that was, is, and ever will be. This concept, difficult to grasp, has far-reaching effects on realisations of time, space, and matter. Suffice it to say that the seen world has often been called maya, an illusion. It is indeed such, an illusion that is essential for the human race to be enveloped in because personality needs that reality in order to relate and experience life on Earth. When that lifetime is finished, the illusion too may finish.

Those who would aspire to follow a path towards the Creator will eventually come up against a barrier to progress. That barrier is created by the mind as consciousness expands beyond the boundaries of earthly experience and doors are opened into a broader field of experience. All experience, before being accepted into the mind, must have a niche created into it into which it can fit. Should the new experience be similar to that which has been previously known, the information is quickly assimilated. Should the experience be new, it has no niche into which it can fit and, therefore, is not accepted. The new information is rejected utterly and completely until the mind creates a cell for it and that new information will only then feel valid to the individual concerned.

The violence with which alien concepts are rejected by the mind is a source of wonder indeed and has created sympathetic tremors throughout the body of many a man, a tremor sufficiently strong as to cause an outbreak of violent indignation. The personality, nearly always seeking reassurance from experience, would hold new information at bay for considerable lengths of time, seeking always to suppress that information and, if necessary, destroying its originators until either that information no longer has any relevance to the individual or until a change in personality may occur, enabling the said information to be at last accepted into a broader reality.

What it takes for mind limited by earthly experiences and concepts to expand into a reality where the values of time, space, and matter are at total variance may be appreciated. For many, such concepts will never exist. For others, they may be accepted as principles for experimentation and quantification, principles never to be resolved into fact. Few in number can grasp the beauty and vitality of permanence based on the concepts stated above and so the barrier remains for many. This stumbling block is a major hazard on the road to God. God is not to be found whilst limitations are a reality. There may well be experiences of exultation, of joy, but the truly explosive nature of exultation and joy that signify the presence of God will remain an illusion

That which cannot be overcome must be lived with. The rewards that await the traveller, as he crosses the divide between illusion and truth, are the certainty that never again can there be a problem, never a cloud, never any fear. Pure joy, forgiveness, and patience are received as the gifts of the spirit. Those who would experience that joy must first prepare themselves to be God's disciples through the trinity of prayer, devotion, and duty, and seek always to penetrate the veil beyond which reality lies. The experiences of life are meant to act as a spur to further endeavour and those experiences are all we have, all that is necessary, for the path to be trod towards that goal.

Pity and understand those who hesitate at the gate between Maya and life. Pity and feel compassion for the brother who has not the courage to forge ahead into the unknown because that brother is part of you – indeed, is you. Therefore, if you would progress yourself, ensure that those whom you meet at the fence are helped over to the best of your ability. Some will not succeed and yet, until all do, the totality that is you and I cannot altogether succeed. Do not think that you may act in isolation. That which you are, your fellow man is also. All are one and where one succeeds, all will succeed. Where the one fails, the failure taints all.

Those whose task it is to bring information to the seekers on the path to God find their role easy or difficult according to whether the seeker has managed to transcend the limitation of his imagination and is able to open his mind to influence by word and by thought. Many and varied are the instruments of the Great Spirit, instruments incarnate on Earth and discarnate in spirit. The message is the same when genuine and should be sifted by the recipient for the gold of truth. Acceptance of information depends upon the abilities mentioned before but misinformation is tantamount to denying God the right to speak and is a grievous sin. And yet, misinformation has been made greater use of in formulating religions throughout the ages than truth.

The power and the principle upon which the foundation of existence is built relies on acceptance by the recipients of that power. Through acceptance is more power ultimately generated to further the onward flow of spirit which drives the machinery of life. Through acceptance does more energy become available to fuel the fires of eternal spirit. Through acceptance is all possible. Should the power be denied, the opposite happens, which could and would have disastrous consequences for the viable continuance of life as we understand it.

If it were not for the vast majority of life mechanisms found throughout the universe accepting blindly the inflowing thrust of spiritual power, then the totality of energy available to precipitate the turning of the spiritual wheel and life would quite literally grind to a halt. Such a condition, whilst unlikely to happen, is a constant threat to complacency and spurs those charged with its ministration and communication never to forget, always, to be alert to the possibility of energy being won or lost in the ongoing battle to win supremacy over chaos and death. It is unthinkable that any situation should be tolerated which would diminish the overall bank of spiritual energy and yet how quickly are whole nations influenced by a powerful mind enwrapped with designs for the downfall of his fellow man which contaminates the minds of those sitting on the fence and so swaying them into areas of disbelief.

The contagion spreads and quickly the balance of power is challenged. At such times, the angelic forces are able to do little to assist in the fight because their weapons, spiritual power, are being depleted by the enemy that they would influence for good. Thus, it is that forces for evil can often hold sway over man for long periods until such time as, one by one, little by little, souls are influenced for the better and a tiny amount more of power is regained, leading ultimately to the victory of right over wrong. Victory, though assured, is ever hard won and inevitably there are forces envious of the power that the evil group once held and hopeful to rule through chaos themselves who set about gaining support from their contacts and so the battle commences again in another theatre of war.

Would it were that man could live at peace, one with another, however, man has free will, freedom to choose, and the right to take the path to destruction should he so choose. It is beholden upon the angels of mercy to correct and redress any imbalance in the power structure resulting from the actions of those individuals so that the overall tenor of the spiritual climate is fair. The task of monitoring, administrating, and distributing spiritual energy is placed at the disposition of trusted angelic hosts who work as a hierarchical team, causing energy to rise and descend through the realms of existence according to the needs of those realms. Such beings are not capable of being described in any terms meaningful to man incarnate and, indeed, few souls discarnate are able to comprehend the existence of such.

However, these precepts do exist, are real, are active, and essential to the ongoing realities of life as man would experience it. They are not God. God is the creator. These are His servants. Their nature and their structure within the concept of life is bizarre in our terms. Life has many forms and the life of these creatures follows a different scale indeed from that of any human being. It is generally imagined by man throughout the ages that the angelic forces and God Himself resembles man. It is stated in the Bible but it is not necessarily true. Angels there are who resemble man though, generally, the angelic forces described throughout the old and new testaments that have been passed down to us today describe, more likely, discarnate souls returning to fulfill an obligation made to assist the next generation of their tribes.

The true angelic hosts have no interest in man, are not human, at least in any way that resembles a man, and have different objectives to their existence, more broad and far-reaching than any man could conceive. They are the engineers of life. They ensure that all is in order that the dramas of life might be played out by us lesser mortals without upsetting too much the balance of spiritual power upon which the balance of all depends. These angelic forces, however, are real. The reality to which they conform is not ours but our reality is but an illusion within greater realities, themselves illusions within far greater realities. This process goes on until all is an illusion except the one great truth. Nevertheless, the angelic forces are very real within their own sphere and play an ever-increasingly important role in an atmosphere where man wars increasingly against God and his fellow man and in an environment where the destructive capacity of man has reached unprecedented limits.

Those who would aspire to achieve results in seeking the kingdom of God and those who would use the power so released would do well to consider the price that must be paid in total sacrifice and struggle by themselves and by others who would assist them in their travails. The cost is dear indeed because the price is total surrender to the power of God, total abnegation of ego and personality to the will of the One, and surrender of all pride, desire, and emotion to that one power which demands all and in return offers nothing, nothing except that the individual is able to appreciate the beauty and splendour, the peace and happiness of being at the Godhead. These goals all men purport to seek and, indeed, only a fool would reject and yet most are so entrapped in the Maya of life that they are totally unable to appreciate the reality awaiting them.

It is of paramount importance that seekers after spiritual knowledge should prepare themselves both physically and mentally for the journey that they must undertake. The road is long and the way arduous. Spiritual work makes great demands upon the physique due to the fact that in order to gain or receive spirituality, an exchange has to be made in terms of the vital power that is related to the body. An exchange signifies that, to receive, it is necessary to give. The receiving of spiritual blessing implies that the receiver gives a certain portion of his physical power, the power that would normally be used to sustain and regenerate the body.

Power, once given, is lost at least for the time being and that leaves a vacuum in terms of power. The vacuum is filled with spirituality. The spiritual power once received is equivalent to the physical power lost and restores balance in a physical sense. The spirituality of the individual has, of course, risen by that degree by which spiritual power has been absorbed. However, the danger point is during the period when energy has been given and the body is depleted, awaiting fulfillment by the Holy Spirit. At such times, the person concerned is in a weak condition and is open to all manner of illnesses and infections which can take hold during such times.

It is advisable for the student of the mysteries of life only to aspire to receive spiritual power at times when he is feeling fit and well and at times when sleep and rest may be gained at will. If, during the long journey towards perfection, a person incarnate attempts to perfect himself and yet still makes the normal demands upon his body that employment and the home environment make, there is a real danger of the body becoming overtaxed and serious illness and even death of the body occurring. The advice given to the student is to plan his voyages in stages and listen to the dictates of his body so that he does not overtire himself. Thus it is that many who made great progress during their earthly incarnations found their life force shortened.

This is unfortunate when it occurs as there is much to be gained by an earthly incarnation, a fact often only realised once that incarnation has terminated. It is sad to shorten it through overexertion which, to a certain extent, defeats the object of attempting the voyage. However, having stated the dangers on the path, the rewards will be considered and they are many. Such is the value of the blessings accrued through having achieved certain progress along the way that any effort made to reach that goal is worthwhile. The blessings, whilst themselves taken individually may appear insignificant, are nevertheless vital and wonderful progressions towards perfection.

The steps can be appreciated in hindsight and are noticeable in that the problems that one was bound with gradually lift and are diminished in proportion to lessons sent from the Almighty for the betterment of the recipient. Peace of mind is an adjunct to progress and finally bliss. A state of at-oneness is achieved. There is felt no desire to escape from perceived realities of life as there are with drug-induced enhanced states. Indeed, involvement with aspects of life relevant to the progressive needs of the student is essential to the achievement of these goals. There can be no progress without sacrifices and spiritual sacrifice is not the killing of an innocent animal nor is it drinking wine or eating bread. Sacrifice implies that the individual must be brought to the altar and should suffer. The suffering, which is nearly always in the form of service to God made manifest in man, results in a reward being made by God through acceptance of the sacrifice. Reward, of course, has been mentioned earlier. Thus, it is that service in any way, shape, or form is considered a necessary part of the spiritual path.

Some factions would attempt to achieve perfection by total withdrawal from life. This path has its adherents  and the act of withdrawal is, in itself, a heavy penalty to pay for the rewards gained because it is unnatural for humans to live a solitary life and so that sacrifice is rewarded by the granting of blessings. However, one feels that the path is rather a negative and passive way, not perhaps conducive to the furtherance of the human race on Earth and thus perhaps not to be regarded as a path most suited for the vast majority to follow.

A more promising avenue to the future would be total involvement with aspects of life chosen by God for that individual where that individual would be most able to serve and be most able to benefit by service. Service done for the benefit of financial profit brings no reward. Service performed for God, even when rewarded financially, is accepted by God and confers blessing upon the worker. And so, the advice given to any individual contemplating progression towards perfection would be to seek the guidance of Almighty God in obtaining a suitable arena of service and, once that has been attained, to devote himself ardently to serve mankind within that arena to the best of his ability and to rest assured that that labour will be accepted as sacrifice upon the altar of service by God. His blessings will follow in due course.

Commensurate with service should come devotion. Devotion implies that the individual subjects himself to a higher being and recognises that that being is capable of receiving that devotion and is able to confer blessings upon the devotee as a reward for the devotion given. The process is a dual one. It is a giving out from the devotee to the devoted one and a receiving by the devotee. That which is given in a period of devotion is, in fact, the power that would normally have been used to fuel the fires of personality and ego, power that would have been used to strengthen the bonds of earthly ties. Having given that power to the Almighty, the giver receives, in return, spiritual power which raises and strengthens the spiritual concept of the individual. Thus, gross matter has been transmuted into spiritual gold.

This process is vitally necessary for the individual concerned. His future in all respects depends upon the change that occurs. Should devotion not be practiced as a daily ritual, then any other spiritual activities undertaken would be harmful to that individual. Spiritual work makes demands that only spiritual power can satisfy. Spiritual power alone is sufficient to transport the voyager along the path towards perfection. Therefore, it must be stressed that regular periods of devotion are necessary and must become daily routine for the disciple of God. Stress must also be placed on the need to consider the physical body at such times and care taken to minimise physical and emotional exertion at the times mentioned previously when the body has given up a certain portion of physical power and it has not yet been replaced with pure spiritual power.

There is need also to consider one's emotional stability at such times. The turbulence created in mind during early endeavours towards perfection are great. Stability, albeit tenuous, is achieved as a compromise by most individuals prior to feeling the need to find God and, once new routines are firmly established, stability returns once again. During initial periods of spiritual endeavour, sweeping changes are wrought throughout personality which causes much turbulence and emotional discomfort. Indeed, it is not uncommon for people to experience emotional breakdown at such times. This should not occur, however, if the path is followed with care, considering always the feelings of the body. Emotional trauma is, however, a prerequisite to receiving spiritual blessing and the student should be prepared to experience it to a degree and adjust his work, devotion routines, so that changes happen slowly and without drama.

Taking stock of the information imparted so far and assimilating that information into the subconscious will cause changes to be wrought in the personality of the student. These changes, though subtle, will begin to allow a process of expansion of mind to occur, the results of which will be a fruition of inventiveness and a process of creativity which is indicative of the beginnings of wisdom. Wisdom is a word often used by individuals where the correct word would be cunning. True wisdom is not acquired through experience of life alone nor is it achieved through academic knowledge. Power, when acquired, does not bring wisdom as a handmaiden.

Wisdom is a process of merging worldly experience with soul growth. The result of that activity is to create a person who has the ability to make decisions and to act upon them to influence others, not for financial, political, or theological gain, but to act in a manner that implies godliness, transposed into an earthly environment. Such actions are not coloured by selfishness but are the epitome of selflessness moulded upon reality. Few decisions taken in the world today or in the past use such criteria as process for action, and few individuals could genuinely be called wise. However, as with all gifts of the spirit, wisdom is open to all. Intelligence, though important, is secondary to spiritual growth and it is spiritual growth that decides a person's wisdom. The process of acquisition is long and requires diligent application by the student before it is released into his custody, but, like all gifts of the spirit, it is worth gaining and as soon as possible.

The manifestations of perfection are such as to leave no doubt upon the disciple that perfection is being achieved. So that there can be no doubt in the heart and mind of the inquirer as to his progress along the path, there are placed certain milestones to guide him, to remind him of the distance travelled and to act as a warning that the traveller has not arrived at his destination. The past is strewn with the debris of past endeavours and should be picked over with great caution. Past endeavours, whilst themselves valuable at the time, bear no relation to that which will be necessary in the future and should be left on the path, shunned, with one's face always turned to the light, the eyes only upon the goal. Disciplines relevant to today's exercises need not necessarily apply tomorrow for, as the student progresses further from the land of Maya and further into the reality, so the rules governing his actions within those spheres alter.

Christ was not bound or limited by the laws of nature that applied to the uninitiated. Initiation brings with it nothing except the knowledge that the initiate has much to learn and initiation confers no special rights upon the individual. Indeed, it infers great obligation towards the group with whom he would travel and from whom he receives knowledge. Initiation is a responsibility that binds an individual to his group and is the first step towards remitting his sense of isolation with the possibility of confirming oneness with the group.

To all concerned, it is clear that individuality is only a temporary measure created by personality and is intended to endure only as long as it takes for that personality to realise greater realities. Then the step can be made freeing him from isolation and liberating him into the warmth of multiple souls acting as one. This state, strange in concept, is a most blessed achievement and brings with it assurance and peace.

However, as with all things, there is a price. The price is devotion to God - suppression and replacement of earthly emotions and earthly opinion and a willingness to resist not the flow of the group. It might be questioned as to how a person would be able to operate in what appears to be isolation whilst his personality is responding to a group pressure. That question, if asked, infers total lack of an understanding of initiation. It is in fact quite possible to carry out one's duties each day, responding to the pressures of life, and, at the same time, making decisions on a group basis. Not mine, but "thy will be done". This state has been mentioned before cannot be conceived by one immersed in the world of illusion. It is obtained by those of elevated consciousness.

# CHAPTER 2 - SPIRITUAL GROWTH & MEDITATION

The concept behind a belief in a deity is one that is being contrasted with a pseudo-scientific analysis of the creation of life and matter. There have been, from time to time, groups of intelligent yet ignorant people who have intellectually manipulated the evidence presented to their faculties with a view to determining with finality the reason as to why and how matter came into being. The arguments put forward by those people are convincing to those content to limit their investigations to the visible and near visible. They arrive at hypotheses by a method of deduction containing errors of limitation and misunderstanding.

It is not possible to view the world through a telescope nor yet a microscope and observe all of creation. Instruments do not exist that can quantify the immensity of creation in all its forms of manifestation. Those who are prepared to ignore what they cannot see, touch, or measure will be forever limited to a false concept of creation. However, their methods of investigation are basically sound and will in time lead them or others to the conclusions that matter and life exist outside of their abilities to quantify.

In a true investigation of God's kingdom, for the power of God does indeed exist, man is fully equipped with all that is necessary to view, quantify, and understand the true limits of creation. He's equipped with a brain, a mind, and a soul. Those three instruments will, if used correctly, open every door to every corner of creation. Learning to use those instruments is even more difficult than learning to use even the most complex of scientific apparatus for the key to investigation of truth is letting go of self.

Man is conditioned, since birth by an acquisitive society, to measure progress by amassing around himself possessions, qualifications, and wealth which are regarded as a measure of his stature. Education concentrates on development of intellect and awards prizes to those most successful. Man is heading, with ever greater momentum, away from truth and reality. A process of reversal is necessary before a true investigation of life may begin. It is necessary that possessions are regarded as props to comfort and not rewards for success achieved. Academic qualifications and respect of one's intellectual abilities must be seen to be the empty rewards for description of a life of illusion.

It is necessary to become as a child again to enter the kingdom of Heaven. Do you think that God would take any perverse pleasure in concealing His universe from man? He created man and man comes fully equipped to realise all that is. Once one appreciates that nothing at all, in a material sense, is required then one can question in which direction one should proceed to unlock the doors of the mysteries. One may always be assured that in every investigation involving a voyage of discovery into God's kingdom that the answers to any questions, the solution to any problem is already at hand. The tools used to uncover these answers are there and so it is merely necessary for the investigator to apply himself in order for all to be revealed.

The process to be gone through is always and ever the same – meditation on God. That simple act, if assiduously performed, will in time provide all answers to all problems throughout all time. It must at all times be borne in mind that all of history, all the mysteries of the world are able to be contacted and appreciated by every student when the development of simplicity in faith permits it. Let us, therefore, be content to view life from the level that we find ourselves and instead of devoting time and effort to the intellectual pursuits that will ultimately prove futile, instead devote our energies to unfolding the powers of God latent in us and the wonders of the world will be revealed in glory.

There is a time and a place for all things to occur relating to the infinite complexity of material change and organisation. Those who would aspire to understand each and every aspect of life would do well to liken their travels to the voyager into unknown territories. He should prepare himself as best he may by planning each step in advance and ensuring that he has obtained the necessary equipment and information to ensure success. If preparation is not thorough, success is not assured, and the journey will be hazardous and may end in failure. It is beholden upon each individual traveller to prepare himself and ensure that he is fully able to succeed before he commences.

Anything left undone, anything left to chance, will jeopardise the mission. The traveller must not rely on any other person to assist him or support him. He may well travel in a group but he makes the journey himself by his own efforts. No one will carry him if he stumbles. The others will be occupied in helping themselves. The advice given to any disciple of God is to ensure thorough preparation in every respect and then the journey will not end in failure.

A task for the disciple is to discover what he requires for the journey. Humans basically are complete in themselves for their voyage towards the Maker but because personality plays its part in clouding the light of purity and simplicity, it is necessary to study aspects of personality from the point of view of investigating strengths and weaknesses. Personality defects should be brought to the fore, examined, and steps taken to correct them because they will act as stumbling blocks to progress at some stage. The process of correcting a personality defect simply requires that the fault is identified and a prayer sent to God for that fault to be rectified. Subsequently, each time the fault arises in daily life, it should be brought to the attention of personality, note made of it, and it should be pushed to one side. Eventually, the fault will disappear through lack of nourishment by personality.

It is important that the disciple does not identify with the faulty emotion being considered. It is not a part of soul and as such has no value. The effect must be viewed and shelved, leaving soul and mind unruffled. Gradually, imperfections will leach away, leaving the soul shiny, pure, and whole, unfettered by any shortcomings or disabilities. Then may the journey be commenced. However, it will be noticed that in the degree that personality faults are removed, so the end of the journey comes closer. The student in fact does not travel at all. The path and the goal are one. Personality and its emotions cloud the path and cloud the goal. The goal awaits those who can remove the stains of useless pride, ego, and doubt.

An examination each day during meditation of personality aspects will quickly and correctly reveal those not aligned with the path of perfection and will gradually enable them to be disposed of. The joys of expanded vision will be the rewards of he who can overcome his emotions, and health and happiness will accompany him who achieves genuine success.

Taking into account the various factors relating to the voyage of discovery into the mysteries of life, one should come to the conclusion that matter, time, and space are interrelated and interpenetrate one another. If this is true, then it leads to the conclusion that it should be possible to investigate areas outside of the here and now. For this to become a viable reality, it not only has to be true in principle but accepted by the would-be investigators and also knowledge gained relating to the procedures necessary for the acts to be elucidated. It must be possible, for genuine investigation of the past, present, and future, for limitations of time and space to be overcome resulting in a super human form of contact stretching in several directions simultaneously, if necessary. Thus, if we can accept that the laws of physics concerning these subjects are not totally able to circumscribe reality, we begin to open doors into strange new realities which bear little relationship of limitation to that previously experienced. For, the truth is, that man is God-like, should he realise it, and the kingdom of God is his to explore freely and without limitation once he has accepted God as his father and will allow God and not his own personality to prescribe the limits of his abilities.

It would be pleasant to describe techniques and exercises, mantra and prayers, to open doors into the wider forms of life but, unfortunately, there are none. Neither are there secret societies, clubs, and organisations holding the key nor yet can any stone, colour, perfume, or flame open the door. The path to this newfound freedom is always and ever the same for all people in all aspects of life throughout all time. Spiritual growth is the key. Only by following the precepts given in this publication, which has been repeated throughout the centuries by every prophet and will remain unaltered, can the way be made smooth.

All men discarnate and incarnate have equal opportunity to tread the path and, for those willing so to do, peace and happiness passing all understanding, awaits them. For those unwilling to make the effort, the door will remain closed for it cannot be opened by the will of man. Such is the divine nature of man that he can and should allow the Godhead to shine through him, releasing all his suppressed and latent powers and allowing him to realise his full potential as man made in the image of God. It is, therefore, beholden upon the genuine seeker to pursue the path to God with fervour and in peace in anticipation of the great day when the power of God begins to shine from his soul, irradiating his physical and spiritual bodies with soul power which is unlimited spirit of God. Then may the student rise to become one with the Master.

Let it be understood that life, matter, and spirituality are not concepts that can be fully quantified using just intellect alone. The stumbling block is that matter, for example, a multidimensional substance stretching beyond purely physical bounds into areas that can only be appreciated by those of expanded vision and so, to gain anything like a complete picture, it would be necessary to make statements concerning matter to include data garnished from areas much further afield than the Earth field alone.

However, the situation may be inverted in that a person of expanded vision would, per se, be in a position to make logical and meaningful remarks relating to matter on a number of planes which would include standard statements drawn from the limited laws of physics governing matter here on Earth plane. Such statements would not only include remarks concerning mass, size, shape, and quantity but would include data relating to growth, feeling, and potential. It may seem unrealistic to take, for example, a piece of wood and consider it as a living organism but that is exactly what it is. Even when it has been cut from a living tree, dried, and prepared for use, it still has a potential for emotion and development.

Such factors would be difficult to appreciate by anyone not able to tune into cosmic knowledge but, to those so endowed, it is obvious that all matter glows with life on several planes and the word death has absolutely no meaning here. An exercise relating to developing the ability to expand consciousness might be to take an inanimate object and, by holding it in the hand and by trying to contemplate on it, it should be possible to link with its vibrancy on higher planes of existence, thus demonstrating the beginnings of expanded consciousness. Concepts, questions of interest and moment concerned with developing opinion related with the spiritual planes are resolved only by those who have firsthand experience of those planes. Anything else must be conjecture and should not be confused with fact.

Therefore, it is necessary for any student of the occult, for such is a term we may use to describe the hidden mysteries and is in no way limited to evil, to become familiar with the planes of existence relevant to his immediate and future progress in order that he can fully relate to the laws governing those planes, with a view to mastering the techniques required for manipulation of matter and form for the benefit of others to the glory of God, in order to further the upward flow of spiritual energy which will benefit all man. The techniques required are of no relevance to those unable to reach into the relative spheres and so it would be unwise, foolish, and dangerous for the novice to practice. Those of a sufficiently advanced state of development may begin to explore these new territories and begin to put into practice those techniques relevant to that plane. Then, one may expect results to be achieved which will bring great delight to the experimenter and to those less enlightened.

We now elucidate graphically the techniques to be followed by the student wishing to operate in what is termed the astral body. This body, like all the permanent or more durable bodies than the physical frame, is composed of matter of much finer substance than is found on the Earth plane and is not limited by shape to follow the outlines of the Earth form, the human body. It is roughly ovoid in shape but may change its appearance according to the thoughts, feelings, and desires flowing throughout the heart and mind of the individual. It irradiates colour of various hues and of relative purity. It can glow with brilliance and beauty in a pure soul and can be reduced in intensity and form to a dismal shape and shade in an evil eminence.

This astral body is as real as the physical form, indeed more real, and will outlive the human form by a great deal. All living objects and entities have an astral form and, as everything is alive in one sense, it follows that all things, even a grain of sand, has an astral form. It also follows that the degree in which that astral form is able to manifest itself is dependent upon its spiritual growth and that, therefore, the astral form round a grain of sand is of lesser intensity than that surrounding an advanced soul. That does not imply that a grain of sand is any less than a human. Both have a place in the kingdom of God and, in God's eyes, all are equal.

However, man is normally the most advanced of God's creatures walking the Earth and one expects that man should exude a more vibrant form of radiation in the astral world than would a grain of sand. Therefore, man finds when he is able to transfer his active consciousness into his astral vehicle that he appears to be floating in space. He is, in fact, in an area where the astral forms of all things surround him. If something exudes little light, it appears almost nonexistent and, therefore, there is the disconcerting experience of not having solid matter like the ground, trees, houses, etcetera, for him to relate to. He has, of course, no need of any of these. Gravity does not exist. Temperature plays no part. He eats not. He sleeps not. He requires no shelter from adverse weather conditions. He is a body of light living in a world of light which is his true state and his true home.

Many, however, cannot accept this strange concept and require to have their feet placed upon a form of terra firma. So they create with their imaginations a form of Earthly existence with houses, furniture, trees, libraries, and all they need whilst incarnate. There is nothing wrong in this. It brings them comfort and an ability to identify with their perceived reality. It is, however, not reality. It is imagination brought into the fore. Eventually, they will grow to realise that nothing is necessary for them to experience life in the astral realms. Then they will allow their possessions to disappear and appreciate the joy of standing in God instead of being blinded by illusion.

It is possible and indeed necessary for the student to familiarise himself with the technique for entering the astral realms. As with all spiritual work, until the student is ready, the doors remain closed to him. He will only be able to raise himself into this world when he has developed his own astral vehicle to the point that it is able to support his consciousness. The actual technique of entering the astral plane is very simple. By meditating on God, power is transferred into all the bodies of light surrounding an individual and the astral vehicle will become strengthened to the point where it will support a transference of consciousness to that vehicle.

The student should, from time to time, during his meditation, test the readiness of his astral body to accept him by attempting to pass into that realm by imagining, for example, walking through a door or by using a similar technique. He will discover the method most suitable for himself with experience. What he experiences in those realms will depend on many things. It is a strange world compared to the Earth plane because there is nothing solid upon which one can make datum points of progress. Therefore, initially, it will seem strange and no two people will experience the same thing. Actually, that is true also on the Earth plane but that concept is clouded by the view of reality that apparently solid material creates.

With all solidarity gone, the student will find himself quite literally all at sea. However, he should, at all times, remember that he is not alone and that his helpers, guides, and spiritual masters are never far away. They can be called upon to give assistance at a moment's notice. Also, the student is free to return to his Earth consciousness, should he wish. He will do so automatically after a time anyway because he would be unable to sustain himself in that level for more than a few minutes. It must be reiterated that such work is not for those who have not a firm foundation of sensitivity and is definitely not recommended for anyone who has reason to doubt that he is able firmly to operate in an Earthly condition with satisfaction.

The technique outlined above would be dangerous to anyone taking drugs of any description or alcohol or for anyone who has reason to suspect that he is schizophrenic or has an hallucinatory illness. In fact, he would not achieve the desired result at all. The astral world is open only to those who have earned the right by spiritual development. Anyone else would be deluding themselves and to those in the categories mentioned above, the result could be damage to the psyche and have a completely negative result.

Some people are able to develop a form of astral projection in which they are able to detach their consciousness from within their body and project either voluntarily or involuntarily at a distance but nevertheless are still firmly on the Earth plane. This phenomenon is caused by an astral form close to the body and is normally associated in close conjunction with the body which is able to disassociate itself and is able to wander about, containing the consciousness of the individual. This phenomenon, whilst perfectly normal, is rare and is a useful technique for exploring the lower astral world. It is not a means of entering the true astral realms of light.

The lower astral world is closely related to the physical world and is virtually identical. The forms of all Earthly things are visible and such astral forms can sometimes be discerned by the naked eye. However, gravity, heat, and related matters have no relevance in that realm. Such a state is often confused by those able to exploit it to the actual Earth because there is virtually no difference. However, it is not so. It is the lowest of the astral spheres. There is some danger of meeting lower astral thought forms, often unpleasant, on this plane and it would perhaps be better left for those who are designed by nature and by God to be denizens of that area. The student should concentrate on exploring the higher astral worlds of light and beauty.

Let us, therefore, proceed to define the technique for true meditation on God. Only by so doing is the student able to expand his consciousness and his soul to free him from the trammels of Maya. There are many techniques described by exponents of a variety of philosophies for enabling one to reach perfection. "All roads lead to Rome," it has been stated and we may rest assured that all forms of meditation will open the gates to the kingdom of Heaven. Some techniques urge the student to ignore the gifts of the spirit that may become available as a result of progress achieved and some forms of contemplation seek to immerse the student in the joys of meditation to the detriment of progress.

It is therefore necessary for the student to choose a course of meditation and contemplation which will not only open the gates of Heaven as quickly as can be safely achieved but that will also permit him to unfold the gifts from God that result for the benefit of his fellow man sick through lack of contact with God. The technique of meditation recommended is thus dependent upon the student placing himself in a position to benefit according to the warnings and recommendations outlined earlier.

Assuming that due relevance has been paid to those admonitions then it is recommended that the student place himself in a room on his own with the door shut. A room remote from traffic or neighbour interference is necessary during early stages. Later, the student will be able to ignore any extraneous noise. He should sit comfortably, warm, and quietly close his eyes. After allowing his metabolism to settle for a few moments, he should invoke God's blessing and protection. Then, he should focus his attention upon an imaginary spot of light in front of him, holding that spot of light stationary in his imagination as best he may and recognising that spot of light as the power of God, as God himself.

Initially, it is difficult but will have to become a technique accomplished at some stage in his existence so it is better to master it now. The spot of light should be held for a few minutes initially. As the student progresses, he may hold it for longer periods of time but he should not strain. When he feels that he has meditated sufficiently then he may withdraw his attention, say a benediction to God, and resume his normal existence. This apparently simple exercise will bring great blessings and advancement to the student and is a technique that he may continue to use after he has removed his consciousness from the Earth and has finally entered his true home, the spiritual world.

# CHAPTER 3 - THE ACTS OF THE MASTERS

Those who require to seek into the mysteries of spiritual matters need to have firsthand knowledge of the techniques required to unwrap those mysteries. There can be no real and genuine progress made by any seeker until he has a firm grasp on the ground rules governing matters of inquiry. Let it be firmly understood that speculation and interpolation cannot and must not be mistaken for true knowledge gained by actual experience and that experience can only be gained by those suitably qualified by dint of long and ardent devotion to the path of God, for, that path and that path alone enables one to uncover the hidden mysteries of life.

Many in the past have endeavoured to emulate the master by apeing the acts that those masters were able to perform but none could succeed in duplicating those acts successfully or maintain the deception. Sooner or later, a fraud is bound to be uncovered for there is always someone with sufficiently sharp eyes to observe the falsehood being perpetrated. True acts of a spiritual nature are conducted at a level far removed from the spectrum of the naked eye and the results of such acts, when observed from an earthly standpoint, cannot be construed as fraud as there can be no detection of a mechanism at work. Thus, they are classified as miracles.

Such acts have always astounded the general public when they have been performed because the public have always been educated by orthodoxy to regard miracles as impossible in the day that they were being performed. Scripture is full of miracles happening many years ago and time has added a veneer of acceptability to such acts. They are safely in the past and may be accepted as real and true without being a threat to the susceptibilities of today. Thus, any miracle performed today is considered to be a trick or a chance happening, no matter how convincing that miracle might appear nor how efficacious the result. They are condemned out of hand because they are a threat to one's established preconceived notions of what is and what is not.

This process applies regardless of what age it may have happened in. Miracles performed by Jesus were condemned by the priests of the temples as untrue and yet those same priests accepted the miracles performed by Moses as real. The acts of Jesus today are acceptable and indeed vital signals as to the genuineness of Jesus to the priests and public of today. And yet, who would believe that those same acts were being performed by gifted people throughout the Earth today? Should such a person be discovered, there are some with eyes sufficiently opened as to be able to accept such acts as genuine but the vast majority of people would either ignore or deride such acts.

Those unable to accept that God has the right to confer the gifts of the spirit on those who have earned them are of course free to do as they choose. Often, they are embittered by charlatans and fraudulent mediums who have acted since time immemorial to defraud a gullible public. But, there are always those who are genuine and able to display the gifts from God and it is a pity to condemn the real with the frauds. The genuine mediums of God's power are not concerned by acceptance or otherwise. They have their hearts and minds firmly on the

Godhead and require no acclaim from the public nor from establishment to boost their egos. They perform their acts as they can and for whom they can and leave the rest of the world to accept or reject as they wish.

Such is the nature of life that, no doubt, a suitably famous and genuine medium acting in good faith today and yet being scorned will have his true worth recognised only long after his death to the Earth. The loss is not that of the miracle worker but it is that of those who reject him. They are not ready to have their eyes opened nor are their hearts ready to be quickened by the soul responding to the out flowing power of God and so they sleep, resting in the arms of Morpheus until such times as they can awaken to the realities of life.

Then, and only then, can they become students of the power of God themselves, for the purpose of the gifts of the spirit is to demonstrate to others that God is and that God's gifts are real and vital portrayals of the essence that flows through all mankind and will burst into life, invigorating and elevating him should he allow it so to do. The gifts have then served their purpose and will remain as a tribute to God as another soul awakens to follow the path, for, as previously stated, until all men can reach perfection, none can. All are one and one is all. It is the duty of each man to respond to the call of the soul and to follow that long trail towards God. In due course, the gifts of the spirit will be released into his custody in order that he may demonstrate to others that God is real and so the chain of vitality is carried forward ever and ever into the future.

That is the dream and ideal that each advanced soul works towards and, should it become reality, wars, strife, separatism, illness, and unhappiness would become things of the past instead of, as is at present the case, that these things are reality and miracles are considered to be things of the past. Never let it be lost to the sight of man that the power of God is ever trying to flow through man and will ultimately succeed. What a pity it is to shut it out when by acceptance does so much more become real that is better than that which exists today.

There is another aspect to the study of the development of the gifts of the spirit which must be considered. All too often it is presumed by lay people that anyone who professes to have special powers and can demonstrate them is in some way different from the ordinary individual, it is presumed that some special right to have access to magical formulae has been conferred to them, enabling those people to perform the acts which often are observed to be in contradiction of the norm that would be expected for all individuals and for all matter to conform.

One might question whether such a proposition would have a basis in fact. It is quite true that a person so enwrapped in the power of God as so as to have access to special powers is considered to be a special person and has, indeed, magical powers when compared to the abilities of a person still unfortunate to be engrossed in the illusions of an earthly experience. But, by the nature that applies to all mankind, all men are equal and all men have the latent abilities to perform similar acts. Thus, it may be stated that the powers of a person enwrapped by the power of God and endowed with the gifts of the spirit would be special but that person himself would only be special in that he was a vehicle for such powers, almost implying that the person and the power relating through him were detached, one from the other.

Such is, in fact, the case. The power of God, wonderful though it is, can only manifest itself through beings and objects. Of itself, it can accomplish nothing and can only exist as a principle. When operating through any material thing, be it mineral, vegetable, or flesh, it veritably comes to life and is able to animate all of creation. However, creation has no life of its own, merely the vitalising spiritual power animating it that gives it the appearance of life. So, if that is true, then the powers of the spirit flowing through a developing soul and permitting him to achieve such wonders is not a function of him at all but he is merely a channel through which the power can flow to perform its miraculous function. The individual is relegated to the role of the alchemist stirring a magical potion, the potion containing the power, not the magician.

Similarly, should a person, animal, or object benefit from such an out flowing of power, is it that person benefitting or is it the spirit of God within that person that is the recipient of the out flowing power from another? Is it the spirit of God that receives the inflowing energy and is itself boosted so as to be able to affect, say, a cure in a sick person? It is normally considered that the spirit of God in a person is perfect and that, in some way, an individual can become sick by shutting himself off from the invading spirit power. This must surely be true and yet if it is so, then, by what token can a person be made to respond to the effulgent power being transmitted by a developing healer to heal that person?

In answer to that question and to all others relating to the power of God and its ability to be transmitted as a healing force, it is necessary to enter the realm of existence relative to the level upon which such action occurs. In the case of healing, action is normally taking place in the higher astral realms because it is often in those realms that illness becomes established. Such illness is often initiated by an inability of an individual to adapt to situations in which he considers he is being treated harshly or unfairly by others or has experienced some lack of love or material possession in the past. Many illnesses are instigated by emotions of that type and so discordant vibrations are set up in the relevant aura or body of light. Such discordant vibrations have the effect of stifling the flow of God's power to that individual and, by so doing, will stifle the human body's ability to regenerate itself correctly. So, illness is the result.

If a healer is brought into the presence of the sick person, he goes through the motions of performing a healing service and automatically the power of God acting within and through the healer senses the area of need by the patient and will commence the inflow of power into that region, manipulating matter in the relevant sphere with the desired effect of bringing harmony back into the affected aura. Should this be successful then a cure will be affected. Should the emotional content emanating from a person's personality defects be strong enough and remain, then there will be no cure. The battle will be lost until such times as the sick one reduces the power of personality and allows the power of God to flow.

Those who would find inspiration through prayer and meditation are those who have already established a link between their inner and outer lives, their higher and lower bodies of light. Such people are able to draw upon energies flowing in a two-way direction causing vitality to be magnified in the ever-living worlds of light and reality. Those who have begun to achieve this process may draw encouragement and inspiration from the fact that this process may develop until each state is as real as the other. Then is an individual able to operate in both areas at once, a state akin to having one's feet on the ground and one's head in the clouds.

However, the term "clouds" has come to imply areas of unreality whereas the process that we describe is a process that leads one ever closer to reality. Therefore all students of life should be open to receive the first inklings of awareness that such process may occur in their lives and be ready to receive the heightened state and to give thanks to God that it has happened to them. Then can the condition become ever more firmly entrenched in the conscious and subconscious until it becomes automatic. The condition brings with it great happiness and fulfillment as energy, spiritual energy, flows into the conscious arena of life, sweeping out distrust, dismay, and doubt and replacing it with the God-like qualities mentioned in an earlier chapter of this book.

Were it possible to shorten the steps to God, the steps taken would need to embrace cognitive leaps of consciousness rather like climbing a staircase, but, unfortunately, it is not possible to take shortcuts to perfection and so it is necessary to achieve the steps mentioned here slowly, one at a time, until the old way of life is left behind as past realities pale into insignificance compared to the vivid new realities presented to the consciousness as greater realities become focused upon.

There are definite steps that one must take to realise these heightened states of reality and these steps are the ones that Jesus outlined in his sermon on the mount known to us as the Ten Commandments and as exemplified by his life. It is necessary for all students of perfection to embrace the dictates given into a pattern of reality that suppresses evil and base thoughts so that the void created by rejection of evil may be filled with love and beauty. Make no mistake. It is not possible to live a life that embraces vile and wilful concepts to act in any but a spiritual manner and still be endowed with the qualities under consideration. One must empty oneself prior to the receipt of blessings. The blessings can only fill the void created by rejection of base thoughts. They cannot be heaped on top of a personality already full. The student is therefore urged to study the teachings of Jesus because those teachings are valid statements from an enlightened one.

There have been other prophets from time to time who have received teachings from on high and have disseminated those teachings to the world. The original message contained the elements that the teachings of Jesus contained. However, as is often the case, the message as received by the prophet may be distorted by that prophet's own emotions and therefore may not necessarily be a true account of the information imparted.

Jesus had no such problem as he himself was enlightened and was an originator of spiritual law as defined by those similarly enlightened as himself. The information he gave was from his soul and through his mind, therefore suffering no distortion in the telling. However, a great deal of time has passed since Jesus uttered those pearls of wisdom and much of the information attributed to Jesus today contained in the Bible is a shadow at best of the great truths uttered by the master and, at worst, a fabrication by people of less than good intent. However, the Sermon on the Mount contains purity and is in essence the intent that Jesus uttered.

Those commandments on their own, if followed and adhered to by any person, are sufficient to carry him into the arms of God. There are other truths and other statements which may be added to further assist progress but it is certain that the ten commandments are the thoughts of those who have trod the path, have reached perfection, and who have realised the principles that must be followed. There is no mention in those commandments of absolution from the result of evil deeds. There is no mention of forgiveness of sin by the ritual of confession. The commandments present a picture of absolute responsibility of the individual for his own actions and for his interrelationship with his brother man and his father God.

It is suggested that the student write out in his own hand the Ten Commandments and study and meditate upon them until a) he can recite them by heart, b) he absorbs their meaning into the fibre of his being. Remember that to kill not means to avoid any action that results in involvement or responsibility for the death of any person, animal, hope, or inspiration. How often do we sneer at the attempts of someone weaker than ourselves attempting to achieve success in pursuit of some aim? We kill their desire to achieve. We kill their confidence. Think on the meaning of "thou shalt not kill" and try to live a blame-free life.

Understand the deep concept of not stealing. We know that it is wrong to steal the possessions of another but do we steal other people's ideas? Do we steal the affections that one person is showing to another through jealousy? Do we steal the hopes and loves, the ideas and plans of another in order to make ourselves appear big in the eyes of the world and in our own eyes? How often do we bear false witness by distorting the truth, by discussing the shortcomings of another with a friend or colleague?

We could go on and examine each of the commandments in turn but sufficient has been said to provide illumination for the student. It is more beneficial for one to make one's own interpretation of the commandments and then to resolve to live by them.

Failure is certain initially. If one could live according to the teachings of Jesus without ever putting a foot wrong, one would be on a par with the master. Therefore, it is inevitable that one will stumble from time to time. Failure should not be regarded as damaging. Correct one's thinking where possible. Resolve not to commit that error again and face the world with expectancy to achieve success. Gradually, the old ways will disappear and the new, God-like, ways will take over. As this state is achieved, so one will come to realise ever deeper meanings of the commandments and find ever greater areas for self-improvement. The result of achieving measures of success will be a greater unfolding of the gifts of the spirit, greater happiness and greater awareness of the oneness of all life.

Beware of deceiving oneself. It is very easy to believe that one is acting in a godly fashion through the unfortunate practice of not examining one's true motives. Therefore, a way of life must be established that a) seeks guidance from God, b) permits contemplation and the opening of the soul to divine influence, and c) gives benediction to God for the help received. It is suggested that morning prayer is practiced to establish a link with the divine soul each day, that time is set aside each day to examine the actions taken during that day, and that evening prayer giving thanks to God is practiced. The divine souls that guide man incarnate on Earth will influence the individual to conduct his life of prayer in the manner most likely to bring success and so, gradually, a pattern of life will be set up that enables the individual to ride the highway to God.

To think in terms of right and wrong, of good and bad, of God and devil is to simplify reality to the point where any meaningful discussion would be fruitless. All life is complex. Most subjects and experiences relating to them are complex. There is seldom any situation relating to any matter where the situation may be regarded as black and white. Therefore, it is impossible to describe situations relating to life in simplistic terms and expect those statements to bear the hallmark of purity in truth. Any adamant statement relating to any event or situation should be regarded with suspicion as there are always extenuating circumstances.

Even if all the known facts relating to a matter under consideration are known, evaluated, and discounted, one should be aware that the situation under consideration is only being viewed with limited experience. There are always areas of life beyond the field in which one operates and, therefore, there are areas of reality about which one can have no knowledge, thus preventing a true evaluation of the situation to be made. So, it is impossible to be positive that assurances can be made concerning the reliability of statements made by any living soul. For that reason alone, it is wise to disregard dogma.

However, it is necessary to have some guidelines to follow in order to live one's life to relate experiences into logical patterns of thinking and, certainly, history is not short of adages and commands, statements and implorations, rules and regulations given for the benefit, or otherwise, of man. Jesus himself is credited with many utterances that go unqualified as to how one should behave in given situations. Thus, it is that we have statute books of mighty size and weight regulating every aspect of behaviour in our so-called civilised world.

If account is taken of the animal and plant kingdom, regard seems to be paid to certain modes of behaviour and patterns of events seem to follow given rules. Who could argue that we are better off because of explicit regulations curbing the worst excesses of those who would benefit from cheating and taking advantage of their fellow man? We consider rules, implicit and explicit, are necessary adjunct to the term "civilisation".

As is so often the case, we appear to have a duality, a dilemma. On one hand we have life on Earth, governed by countless statements of explicit intent which we term regulations and laws and, on the other hand, the statement that no one is ever in a position to give, with wisdom, those laws. The dilemma hinges upon the word "wisdom". Wisdom is the most important attribute gained by any living soul and, like most attributes, it is in part a gift of the spirit. It is considered to be not entirely a gift of the spirit because it has to be earned through much effort. However, it can be gained by all men when they are ready to assume the mantle and is barred from all those who have not acquired the spiritual and intellectual growth.

Those who would aspire to be wise would not find it in any book. Wisdom is not knowledge. It is not the gift of any king, government, or university, nor is it to be gained from ascetic acts like fasting and mutilation of the body. Wisdom is found in the degree that the soul directs to the lower bodies of light of man the power of God lying dormant and awaiting the dawn of life. It is soul growth. Man is a twofold creature. He has lower and upper bodies. His lower vehicles are in touch with the experiences of Earth and have a necessary function up to a point. The upper bodies remain unnourished and somnolent until awakened by the call of the soul and the call of the lower vehicles seeking nourishment from the sweet power of God.

As the soul directs the power of God into those higher vehicles, so they glow with vibrancy and are able, in turn, to nourish and elevate the period of the lower vehicles. The result is a growth towards God and the beginning of wisdom. A wise person may be considered to have achieved a balance between Heaven and Earth. This definition may suggest to the student that many of the individuals who have achieved honour and high rank, power, and fortune throughout the annals of time would, by their actions, be regarded distinctly lacking in wisdom. Others there are, the gentle people seldom heard of who would fit the description.

If a wise person can be located, the student would do well to listen to his teachings. They would be of peace, of love, of understanding. They would not be words of war, self-seeking, and fiscal advantage. Wise people there are on Earth, or close to it. They are not to be found by Earthly means however. They do not advertise, they seldom lecture in public places, and they do not boast of their attributes. The student seeking a wise teacher must follow in the footsteps of all students of the mysteries of life before him and pray to God for help, live a life as blame-free as possible, and, eventually, when the student is ready, the master will appear.

That master may be incarnate or he may be discarnate. It makes no difference. Wise people have no limitations placed upon them of time, distance, or language. The student, when accepted by the master, will become aware of the power and greatness that accompany wise ones and will be taught of the mysteries of life. He will also be taught of the limitations that the student is subject to, limitations implicit as a result of the student's own soul development. Then he will realise that the laws forced on man by man are indeed pathetic outside of the limitations that they impose, for, all laws by their nature are restrictive and, as the student himself begins to acquire wisdom, so the limitations and restrictions, man-made and natural, apply less and less.

Laws there must be or else chaos would ensue amongst those whose souls sleep. Directives are necessary for those who are blind. Signs are required for those who are lost. Unfortunately, commensurate with regulations comes punishment for transgressors and with that comes judgement. Then we are back in the old trap of having to judge the actions of others, when we ourselves are not blameless, and inflicting harm on those found guilty. Any person caught in the trap of having to live by those conditions would find it virtually impossible to achieve soul growth.

At the same time that a judge compares the action of a supposed miscreant to a set of rules created by man, he is automatically limiting the possibility, the reality, of an infinite set of situations and variants to that rule which exist outside of the experience of the judge or the lawmakers. Jesus was said to have been judged by Pontius Pilate. For that very reason, he tried to suggest to Pilate that rules applicable to that place and age were only a tiny part of the laws of God and it is God's laws that man should obey as does, without question, every other aspect of life, be it animal, vegetable, or mineral.

Mankind alone sets rules because mankind alone requires to break God's laws. So, we suggest that the instructions for life given by Jesus in the Bible are in line with the laws of God and it behoves all people to follow them. Whether they coincide with the laws of man is not the concern of the student, just as Jesus did not concern himself with the laws of the Hebrews or the Romans. Jesus was crucified rather than admit to any limitations of God's laws and, should it be necessary, the student must be prepared to suffer a similar fate.

The student, once he realises the truth of God's laws, cannot find truth in man's laws and to deny God's laws would be to lie before God. Lying is a sin and, in a wise man, death is preferable to sin for sin brings death to the soul. Physical death is inevitable anyway sooner or later but soul growth is all that matters. It is unwise for anybody to retard soul growth. The wise cannot be unwise. Therefore, crucifixion is better than sin.

It is recommended that the student reflect on these words. They do not suggest that lawlessness is permitted in any degree. Indeed, the opposite is implied. The laws of God require absolute obedience by the student and the laws of God do not permit any act that would be considered antisocial. However, it is suggested that, like Jesus, we judge not the actions of others nor should we be involved in decision-making in acts that restrict the soul growth of others. The student should seek employment in areas where he is not placed in the position of harming others through word or deed and should regulate his social life so as to be at peace with himself, with all life, and so may allow his soul to expand, bringing wisdom into his life.

# CHAPTER 4 - APPEARANCES

Indifference to one's condition is a position assumed by people at opposite ends of the spectrum of spiritual development. On one hand, those who are so undeveloped as to be in a moribund state have not developed the degree of awareness required for judgement to be made concerning states of existence above and beyond that necessary for the retention of life itself. Those people are in a state similar in essence to that of a plant in terms of spiritual progress and would accept without question the rigours of life, the slings and arrows of outrageous fortune, without comprehending the possibility of being able to ameliorate that situation.

Undoubtedly, such people suffer but their suffering is a suffering of discomfort, not the anguish of intelligent souls who realise greater comforts and who find themselves without them. Should one, therefore, feel pity for such a person for he feels no pity for himself? Should one attempt to offer that person comfort when that comfort may in fact cause anguish as he realises that he is without comfort? Those questions are often not asked by those who move with compassion amongst the failures and dregs of our society, attempting to improve the situation of such people.

If they ask themselves such questions, one would perhaps doubt if they could bring themselves to the conclusion that it is better to ignore such people. It is not in human nature so to do and yet, by disturbing the relative tranquility of those whom we consider to be unfortunate, we assume a heavy burden of responsibility for the pain that we cause them by bringing light into their world. They do not ask us to help them. They specifically reject that help. They live by a different set of rules to us. Their existence is valid and is part of the totality of all life.

At some time, of course, they will change. All humans are God-like in nature and the destiny of all humans is to sit upon the right side of God. Therefore, the individuals of whom we speak must too rise to those heights one day. But who is to say when they are ready to assume that path? Certainly not us who cannot control our own lives, who can see no further than the ends of our noses. The dawn of awakening of their souls is in God's hands and we must wait until the individuals concerned come to us for help.

At that moment, we should rejoice, rejoice in the knowledge that another disciple is on the path to God and we must offer what help, gently, we can. Great care is needed as the awakening of that soul is fragile and we must do nothing to damage its progress. Therefore, our help must be tailored to the simple requirements of providing food, shelter, warmth, and God's blessing. Lectures and admonitions should be avoided at all cost.

As for those who sleep still, go amongst them if you will, administer to their physical needs if it brings you pleasure, but do not waste your time in trying to make them conform to your reality. They tread their own path and are content so to do. Do not feel sorrow as you gaze upon them. Imagine how you appear to an elevated spirit. Do not sneer at nor reject them. They are still part of you as is all life. Do not try to rid yourself of them. They have the right to their existence as do you. Accept them for what they are - humans like yourself but further down the spiritual scale. They will achieve your status one day as you yourself will achieve a higher position. Accept them as you accept yourself and all life.

Conversely, there are those of elevated consciousness who care not for the creature comforts of life. Such people are equally mystifying to the ordinary person. They often take the guise of fakir or mystical man living in a remote cave high in a mountain. They may take the guise of a holy man of a western faith, Catholic, for example, and live a lonely life in a monastery or cell carved out of rock. These people, so advanced, so sensitive, and so holy, often appear to be living a life of forced austerity for some particular ascetic reason.

Do not let appearances deceive you. Man needs nothing to be at one with God. Those who have achieved sufficient advancement so as to have realised this are in a position to reject the glamour of material objects and to be at one with the God made manifest in them. Therefore, such souls require no help from you. Should you visit one of them, they do not even require your company as, by being at one with God and themselves, they are automatically at one with all life. They have everybody as friend, neighbour, and brother. They are not lonely.

Should they condescend to see you, it is because they are willing to disturb their peace and tranquility to descend to your level in order to communicate some of their wisdom to you. They have nothing to gain from you and in fact such contact as they have with you is as unpleasant as your experience would be in contacting those of low existence mentioned before. Therefore, do not imagine that the wise ones who live without their creature comforts in any are way lacking. They have transcended the illusions of the Earth and have no further need of any material thing.

It may seem strange that on Earth we are able to view the two extremes of spiritual development. On one hand, we have those who require nothing because they are sufficiently undeveloped as to be outside the spectrum of material things and, on the other, we have people similarly dressed and in an identical state to our eyes who have totally transcended material requirements. Make sure you do not confuse the one with the other. Make sure also that you do not offer your help or advice to either group unless it is asked for. Stay within your own group. There is enough to do.

# CHAPTER 5 - THE CONCEPT OF PEACE

The history of mankind is one long record of war and bloodshed. The history of the animal kingdom is a tale of life being taken by violence in order to preserve the stronger of any two animals. We say that nature is red in tooth and claw. What we mean is that some creatures live by being carnivorous and thus the dramatic way in which they obtain nourishment captures our imagination. In fact, the vast majority of nature lives by peaceful means. Virtually, the whole of the plant kingdom and most of the animal kingdom lives by obtaining nutrients without killing in the accepted sense. However, the imagination of man is captivated by the gory details concerning the hunting methods of the relatively few creatures that are carnivorous.

Nature is, by and large, at peace with itself and one cannot really accept as true the saying that it is red in tooth and claw. It is the imagination of man that fits that description. In his disembodied states, the creature that becomes man on Earth lives without killing. He does not need food. Energy is ingested directly through the auras and, because of the nature of the elements of auras, it is not possible to take the life of a fellow man or an animal. Thus, the concept of killing is limited to the planet Earth and to man and animals in physical form.

However, hatred is a condition not limited to the Earth. It is possible for hatred to exist by man dressed in his bodies of light and indeed there is at least one area of life that has, in association with it, the conditions necessary to promote hatred to the full and those who wish to experience that degree of anti-love are attracted to that area. Of course, as with all emotions that do not correspond to love, the individuals attracted to that area will ultimately turn, once satiated, and reject the concept of hatred in order to find love.

Commensurate with hatred lives fear. Fear and hatred go hand in glove as do peace and love and are in fact the complement, the opposite, of each other. Neither are gifts of the spirits. They are attributes towards which man strives. They are not natural to man either. He is not born with the concepts of fear and hatred within him. They were unknown to him before he incarnated to Earth and they will eventually leave him once he returns home to the spiritual realms. Whence comes the almost universal feelings of hatred and fear so deeply entrenched within the heart of man?

Hatred is a concept unknown to the animal kingdom. They, animals, do not have the capacity to hate and yet they have the capacity to love. Who could deny that a dog has love for his mentor known to us as his master? Certainly, there are vicious individuals incarnate who abuse and ill-treat their pets in the most appalling manner and those pets fear their master but they never hate. It would be a sad day if that concept were introduced into animal consciousness.

Therefore, let us recapitulate and say that fear and hatred within the auras of humans go together, that fear is known exclusively to animals initially and that hatred is known exclusively to man. Thus it is that they come together on Earth. They are encouraged and introduced to man by the complement of the directors of life, the archangels whom we might term the directors of chaos. The function of the directors of chaos is essential to the ongoingness of life but, once they have free reign, then their effect is evil indeed.

So it is that an insidious force is fed into man's heart to cause the greatest degree of separateness from the concept of God possible. God stands for peace, love, beauty, and togetherness. The opposite is war, hatred, ugliness, and separation. At the root of these negative concepts is fear. Fear will separate one group from another and cause one man to attempt to kill another in case he is first killed. Fear is at the heart of distrust, causes barriers to be built, and will ensure that nothing positive can be achieved. And yet, fear is an alien concept to man. It exists only in animal life.

An examination of a human being reveals two creatures in one. His true larger self is entirely spiritual in nature. Man can be compared to an iceberg in the sense that that which is visible to the naked eye represents but a portion of the totality of an iceberg. With man, he has one physical body visible to the naked eye and seven auras invisible to that eye. He also has a soul and a spirit of God. Therefore, if seven-eighths of man is spiritual in concept and knows no fear naturally, how is it that the body can hold such sway over his entirety?

The simple answer is that because with most people the auras are undeveloped, thus, they do not operate effectively and so the human's physical body represents a large part of the makeup of a man. Thus it is that fear can be introduced and hold sway over his emotions. However, if and when that person begins, through prayer, meditation, and devotion to God, to develop his auras, it must be obvious that such concept of fear must be reduced because developed auras, full of the power of God, know nothing of the emotion fear. Thus, the totality of fear in relation to the totality that becomes man reduces. Simple, isn't it?

Why then is the vast majority of mankind held in the grip of fear and hatred? The answer, of course, is that knowledge of man's auras, knowledge of the techniques of meditation, have been kept from man by those in the grip of the power of evil because such power recognises instantly that knowledge of such matters would sound the death knoll for that power and the power of evil, like the power of good, is forever striving to gain supremacy.

Therefore, we have the sad concepts that throughout the world the techniques of meditation are ascribed to fringe religions not applicable to us, that prayer is formulised and emasculated into ritual chanting that touches neither mind nor heart, and that the auras are considered to be figments of the imagination of misguided souls one step removed from the lunatic asylum. The result is manifest in war and crime, unhappiness and decay of the elements of beauty inherent in man. The situation will continue until the climate is altered so that individuals are aware of the auras surrounding them and of the desperate need to develop them.

It is of paramount importance, also, to equate in the mind the concept of freedom in relation to evil. Whilst it is fairly easy for most intelligent people to comprehend that those who are squarely at one with God may be permitted latitude in relation to liberty of action and that, once we know them and trust them, that they will always act in a godly manner, we can relax our vigil over them, set them free to go and act out their existence as they will without causing us any distress, the same cannot be said for those individuals used by the forces of evil.

Which of us can accept that any evil person has the right to act in an evil anti-social manner, causing unhappiness in those areas in which he operates and still be at peace with the concept of allowing him so to act? And who amongst us would be able to comprehend that he has the right so to do?

Teachings from most religious publications exhort on one hand the turning of the other cheek in relation to acts perpetrated by misguided souls and, at the same time, exhort us to deal with those ensnared with the forces of evil. We are encouraged to drive out the devil from souls of those in his grip, to exorcise people and, in short, to take action to remove the devil and his power from people as far as we can. Is this action valid? Does not the devil have a right to exist if we consider that he too must have been created by God? Does anybody acting in an anti-social manner not have the right so to do? What should the position taken by a true disciple be?

Well, in an ideal world, there would be no anti-social acts and the devil would not exist. We state at once that such a condition will never obtain because it is not part of God's master plan of life to be. The concept of the opposite of God was created by God and is an essential part of God's creation. Without the negative forces, there would be no world, no people. Nothing could exist without the yin and yang – the opposing forces to which we must strive to achieve a balance.

Once again, we find that generations of souls throughout the world have been misguided by the orthodox religions and by philosophers who really should have been able to accumulate sufficient information so as to arrive at the truth. But they have not. And so we are in a position of trying to re-educate mature souls who consider that complete domination and vanquishing of the negative forces would create a Garden of Eden.

Such is not the case. We must always have the forces opposing each other. This is because the forces of good and evil act automatically and blindly. We do not wish to offend the sensibilities of those who visualise God as a man with a white beard and those who assume that God must be infinitely wise, but we feel obliged to present the truth. God was represented with human attributes by those who realised that simple man could not comprehend an abstract force. It is only recently that man has begun to comprehend and quantify the nature of gravity. So can you imagine if an angelic being had suggested to those living long years ago that it was necessary to obey certain rules but the creators of those rules was a blind force? Probably, there are whole communities today who could not or will not recognise such truth.

However, it matters not. We present the truth as we see it and as we know it in our hearts so to be and we permit anyone who disagrees the latitude so to do. The power of God is a force that pulls towards the concept of creativity in all its variation quite automatically and without ceasing. Should there be no opposing force, then chaos would obtain. Matter would combine together endlessly until the universe was full of one enormous planet. Any life force in the nature of plants and animals would live and never die, would procreate until the surface of the planet was choked with living things. In short, life as we know it could not be. So, we need the negative force to limit the power of good, to slow down the rate of growth of reproduction. The power of evil acts as the dustman (trash man), the undertaker of life, disposing of the dead and dying, so making way for the next generation.

Like the power of God, the power of evil acts quite automatically and without ceasing. If there was no power of God, then chaos would ensue in the opposite direction. Life would die out. Planets would decompose into their constituent parts and life would cease. Therefore, we hope that you can understand that life is a balance on a knife edge between the two opposing forces.

The problem is that unless action is taken constantly by those on the side of good, the power of corruption quickly gains the upper hand. Imagine a house standing anywhere on the surface of the Earth. Once built, it begins to decay and the owners of the house have a constant duty to repaint the wood, repoint the brick work, repair the roof, etcetera. Or within a short space of time, nature reduces it to rubble. That is not malign. It is the natural negative force unconsciously at work ensuring the breakdown of all that is. That is its function and it performs it well. The workers for the power of good may be likened to the owner of the house. He has constantly to work just to repair the damage wrought by nature. Should he wish to improve the house in terms of making it larger or more beautiful, he has to put in still more effort and then that requires even greater effort to keep it in pristine condition.

From that example, you can see why, from time to time, great spirits like Jesus come to Earth to exalt all who will understand, all who will listen, to take up the fight against evil. We hope you can understand why you too must take up the fight.

To return to the point originally under discussion, should we prevent any person from acting for the negative forces? Can we answer such a question and yet answer it we must in order to help clarify our position in relation to the pull of opposing forces. We could take the point of view that we should kill any person acting in an anti-social manner and yet, instinctively, we know this to be wrong. But why is it? It would solve the problem by removing from the face of the Earth any person acting in an anti-social manner and projecting them into an area of the spirit world where they might cause distress to those of like mind to them but would not offend more elevated souls.

But our duty to God and man must always be positive. The act of killing is a negative force and therefore comes under the jurisdiction of the devil. Therefore, should we kill, we act for the devil and, by definition, in opposition to God. Similarly, if we imprison or punish, torture or maim, we are acting for the force of evil. So the miscreants go free and still walk the Earth and still cause distress to those whom they contact. Can we do nothing to ameliorate the situation? I am afraid that the answer is no, in a physical sense. We must not touch them.

However, all is not lost. We have on our side the power of God which may be magnified to any required degree through the trinity of prayer, meditation, and devotion to God. That power may be unleashed against those harming us and our fellow man. It is done in the following manner.

Sit down quietly. Visualise the individual and/or the cause that is damaging to peace in the world. Then pray to God in simple language for that person or that organisation to be helped by God. When you have finished, thank God for the power that has been sent to ameliorate the situation. Did Jesus not ask you to pray for your enemies? We ask you to do the same. Having placed those enemies in God's hands, you must leave them there. Do not carry out any action to restrict them. The power of God will enter their hearts and will reduce the action of the power of evil and so their anti-social actions will reduce.

By a similar process, the actions of the controllers of power in the world may be modified. Those of whom we spoke earlier who act in the capacity of judges, politicians, educationalists, trade unionists, etcetera, and who effectively are in a position to be manipulated by the negative force can have that action reduced and changed for the benefit of all. The task, of course, is monumental. People held in the grip of an evil force will not lightly be released by that force. The task of prising evil out and goodness in can be imagined by those on the side of good. The numbers of people acting for the power of good through the action of prayer and meditation is very small compared to the numbers held in the sway of evil.

But, nevertheless, a start has to be made somewhere. The start was made many years ago by the first prophets and wise men to incarnate and there is a vast army of souls discarnate who pray constantly for peace. Therefore, when you join us in prayer for peace, you will be joining a mighty throng. Do not feel isolated. You might be the only one in your house or in your street and yet you join in automatically with the minds of those incarnate throughout the world and those discarnate in the spiritual realms who, like you, pray for peace.

The power of God is sent winging on its way to enter the hearts of those who sleep and waken them to the reality of life and truth. Do not be dismayed by the stories appearing in your newspapers. They merely tell of the actions of those who have not yet been won over to the side of good. The newspapers do not mention those who do not commit crime because the power of God resides within their hearts. Soon the time will come when man will see the crimes committed by those who control them. The worm will turn.

At such times, it will be natural for those newly enlightened to seek revenge themselves for the long years of suffering wrought on them by the few who held power. There must be no revenge. Let God deal with the perpetrators of those crimes as he will deal with the perpetrators of all crime. Do not allow the peace within your hearts to be disturbed by thoughts of revenge. You would only be acting to strengthen the hand of the force of evil. Act always for God in peace and love. Then, by your example, may all learn to follow the path of peace.

Within the context of the study of the human aura, mention was made of force fields surrounding an individual which we term auras. These force fields are pure energy, pure life, and, as such, may respond to the total energy or life force being emitted from a person through his emotions. Therefore, it is noted that the auras may change colour but, much more importantly, any individual reacting to the environment surrounding him will be raising or lowering the vibration rate of those auras and thereby transmitting or absorbing energy.

Those who are influenced by the dark forces are used to manipulate people and situations to create an atmosphere of dismay, despondency, and despair. The effect obviously is to succeed in reducing the vibration rate of your auras as they respond to the vibrations surrounding them. They reduce in value and in hue, and matter is reabsorbed into those auras and that allows a process of destruction to occur. The result may be an accident, a fire, an earthquake. It depends upon many things but you may be sure that if you feel depressed, you will be contributing to your own downfall and also to the downfall of others.

Similarly, any of the anti-Christ emotions, greed, jealousy, hatred, envy, etcetera, will produce negative results and will affect life both close to you and, maybe, far away as you reduce slightly the total energy for creation that is available. It must be clear then that each and every person incarnate and discarnate must strive to be happy, cheerful, and to be full of the positive, Christ-like emotions of peace, love, understanding, compassion, etcetera. The result will be an increase in the total energy available for the world to be at peace. Then accidents, hatreds, wars, and other upsets will reduce.

The problem, of course, is how to be at peace in a world where we are surrounded by negative forces. For a start, you will not be at peace if you identify with the things of the Earth. The satanic forces influence the minds of many who work in areas of advertising and management to create within society a feeling of lacking. It is a condition resulting in one trying to "keep up with the Joneses". The situation is manufactured to make you feel that you are in some way missing out on that which you should have as a result of the effort that you have put into life. Why should you have an old car when all around you appear to change theirs every year? Why should you stay at home each summer when your friends, or enemies perhaps, travel to exotic places in the fruitless search for fulfilment? We could go on to include houses, household appliances, clothes, employment prospects. The list is endless. New areas of creating dissatisfaction are being explored continuously.

The effect, of course, is manifest and manifold: the vast amount of resources in terms of oil, timber, metals, and oxygen that are consumed to create the objects of desire; the vast amount of suffering by those who design, manufacture, and sell these often needless articles; the incredible amount of envy generated by those unable to obtain the goods and the awful disappointment when the effects, being finally obtained and on realising that they were not needed at all are shoddy in quality and do not create lasting happiness and contentment. The degree that the dark forces advance by such practice is awesome.

The counterattack must be complete rejection of the materialistic way of life. If you need a reliable vehicle then purchase one and make sure that it is a solid, well-built vehicle and resolve to keep it for many years. If you need a holiday then seek out a peaceful retreat in a quiet country area and relax. If you need a house then purchase one that you can afford and live in it in peace. Reject this chaotic way of life and you will find contentment within yourself that no amount of chasing after rainbows will bring you.

Do not worry about promotion at your employment. Serve your fellow man as best you can and leave your employers to chase their fortunes. Do not act in concert with them. They are lost and do not know where they are going. In fact, they go nowhere. Leave them to be like dogs chasing their tails and walk the road to God in peace and tranquility.

Meditate every day. Pray every day. Serve God by serving your fellow man. Have respect for the spirit of God inherent in every atom of everything that you use. Do not discard old clothes merely to buy new ones. The same spirit of God is in both. Do not discard vehicles to buy new ones. The spirit of God is in both equally. Serve God manifest in all that you have and try to be at peace with what you have. By doing so, you will change from the lost soul that you may be now to the son of God that is your destiny. Find peace within your heart. Keep peace within your life. Show peace upon your countenance and be sure that, when people look at you, they will be looking upon the face of God.

# CHAPTER 6 - DIET FOR HEALTH & SPIRITUALITY

*Now, before I start this chapter, I need to clarify one or two points. The person from The White Brotherhood who dictated this entire book to me, and you must remember that it was done using clairaudience or channelling as it is sometimes called, asked me if I could make a list of all the fruits, nuts, and pulses that I could find and he would tell me into what category they fitted.*

*Now, when this book was being dictated some 30 years ago, internet did not exist and the only source of information on food that was available to me was through diet and cookery books. So, I went through as many as I could and I made a list. However, I was never really satisfied that I had compiled all the food that was available at that time and, with the passage of time, no doubt there are more exotic foods available now than were available then.*

*I must also say that the names of certain fruits, etcetera, changes according to the country. For example, in England, we have red and green peppers. In America, they are known as bell peppers and so on.*

*So, I have removed the actual list of foods for various signs of the zodiac until I can get a modern update from my guides that conforms to food available today. Then I will complete this chapter.*

*Also, the way clairvoyance works is that I have to have the words already in my mind for the guide to speak them to me. If I do not have knowledge of a word, they cannot make it sound in my mind. So, even if the person dictating to me knew of other foods, if the name of that food was unknown to me, I would not be able to pick it up.*

*And, on the subject of language, you may have noticed, if you have followed the book thus far, that the language used is very formal, precise, and a little old-fashioned. Although I had a reasonable education at school, The White Brotherhood asked me, before commencing this book, to read classic literature and pushed me to return to evening classes studying English in order to advance my vocabulary. Thus, I was able to capture this rather stilted language accurately but I do appreciate that it is not the most easy reading. Bob Sanders.*

*Now, I'm going to get on with the chapter. So I begin.*

The next item to be discussed of interest and concern to the student relates to the subject of diet. There have been many factions over the years that have considered nourishment of the human body in terms of calories, fats, carbohydrates, etcetera, with the view to obtaining a balanced diet. A balanced diet assumes that a person is imbued with the necessary elements to sustain him in perfect health and so it is that, over the generations, learned people have proposed that certain foods in certain quantities should be consumed at given times of the day and expected that all would be well.

However, as is now history, all was not always well. People became ill despite administrations of do-gooder dieticians and so, gradually, the dieticians changed the diet as it became apparent to them that certain foods were inimicable to the human frame and still people became sick. It is also interesting to observe the diets proposed at any particular time by so-called experts from around the world, in China, Russia, Scandinavia, etcetera. At the same moment in time, in different parts of the globe, experts were and are propounding the absolute virtues of a diet widely differing from that being proposed by a fellow dietitian in another segment of the world. It makes no difference. Their patients still succumb to illness and still die prematurely from diet-related diseases.

Is it, therefore, possible to discover a true diet that will bring the necessary vitamins and minerals in their correct quantities to promote a healthy existence whilst, at the same time, avoiding ingesting toxins that cause harm to the metabolism? The answer is, yes, but that answer must be qualified by certain statements and by qualities concerning life in general. The subject of diet is long and complex and cannot be dismissed simply by listing a few items to be eaten and a few items to be avoided. The subject covers a much wider field than the food names alone.

It is necessary to realise that humans are affected by the rays that dominated at their birth and that will affect their progress during all of their existence. Those rays were present in a person's reality long before he was born to Earth and will see him to the Godhead]. The rays, of which people generally know little except in terms of signs of the zodiac, are a vital part of a person's metabolism and affect that person during every moment of his life. It is not the moment to discuss these rays as that, too, is a complex subject and requires much study to comprehend.

It is mentioned in order to elucidate that people may be formed into groups according to the sign of the zodiac. The rays that affect and carry them along the path to God do not only affect humans. They also affect plants and animals. Those who would eat well would do well to realise that food differs according to the rays with which it is in harmony and that, by eating food amicable to him, he will be eating the correct food for him. Therefore, it can be obvious that, before an individual can hope to ingest the correct types of food for his metabolism, he needs not only to know and to appreciate the rays he travels under but also has needs to appreciate the different types of food vibrating or corresponding to that same ray in order that he may appreciate that which is safe and advantageous for him to consume and that which is an anathema to his system.

Such information is vital to his well-being and so it will become necessary for the student to appreciate the finer details relating to his birth sign and to the corresponding rays through which food relates to him. Should he be unable to follow that precept, he is in the position that the vast majority of humanity find themselves in, that is, they are both nourishing and poisoning themselves with every mouthful of food that they eat.

Thus we realise that the subject of diet can be quite complex and that no two birth sign groups of individuals may partake of exactly the same types of food. Those who ignore this fact must continue to nourish their body in the haphazard fashion that they already do but those who can appreciate the validity of this advice will notice an improvement in the health of the body which will reflect throughout their spiritual bodies as well. Thus they will greatly benefit from the dietary changes they effect on themselves.

Should there be any reason why an individual cannot follow the dietary advice given, then that person should follow the guidance of his doctor because some there are with certain deficiencies in their metabolisms who would require supplements of certain minerals or vitamins. Such people should follow the correct diet as far as they are advised to do and follow the directions of a qualified medical practitioner after. Let it be clearly understood that the advice given will benefit all mankind and should be followed scrupulously in order to reap the benefits from it.

It is the general custom amongst vast numbers throughout the world to base their diets upon the consumption of animal flesh. It has been considered, since time immemorial, to be necessary to the human condition despite many peoples throughout that same world living successful lives as vegetarians for economic or religious reasons. A veil is drawn by the meat-eaters over the successful sustaining of life on vegetables alone and meat-eaters join together to convince each other that killing animals is both vital and excusable because life cannot be successfully maintained without it. Reasons are given that man has always been an omnivore since he lived in caves. His close relation, the monkey, is known to eat meat.

And so the argument is conclusively set that meat-eating is required by the human form. And why not? It tastes nice, it makes an attractive centre to any meal, it opens up countless culinary possibilities, and so on. There is a valid reason as to why humans incarnate on Earth should not eat meat, unless, and only unless, they are in danger of starving. It is excusable to consume the flesh of a freshly killed animal in order to preserve the temple of the body because a human body is of a higher spiritual order than that of an animal and, in the balance of spiritual power, it is more valid that a human should survive than an animal. But that is the only reason for killing and for eating the flesh of any animal.

Most human beings on Earth today are not starving and so, to them, it is stated with the utmost force and vigour that they should cease forthwith to kill and to eat God's creatures because they are harming themselves physically and spiritually and, furthermore, are upsetting the balance of spiritual power that the archangels strive so strenuously to maintain. Meat is harmful to the human form. It contains toxins that poison the body. It begins to decay in the body before being evacuated thus creating more toxins and, worst of all, it replaces in the diet some foods that should be eaten in order to maintain the individual in vibrant health.

Meat contributes nothing but harm to the body. It is not necessary and meat contains no mineral or vitamin benefits that cannot be replaced by vegetables, fruits, and nuts. The digestive tract of humans is formed for the digestion of vegetables. Thus, it is long. The digestive tract of carnivores is short so that they may extract the necessary vital elements and excrete quickly the waste matter before it begins to putrefy. The converse happens in humans. Thus, a number of ailments are brought into condition where they could be avoided.

Secondly, there is a complex relationship between the spiritual quality of an animal and the spiritual quality of humans. Whilst it is quite possible to blend the aura of the pet animal to that of its friend or so-called owner, it is not possible to blend the aura of an animal killed against its wishes and in abject fear with those of the individual who consumes that animal with the remnants of that aura still clinging to the meat. A complex pattern of upset is formed in the aura of the eater which may result in strange sensations affecting the emotions of the eater, emotions of violence, hatred, or fear, reflecting the conditions emanating from the meat eaten and moulding into the personality of the eater. Thus, it has been written that meat-eating can inflame the passions, hence the mystique that some foods have with reference, for example, to being aphrodisiacs. That is why certain tribes in Africa would kill and eat the flesh raw of a lion prior to going into battle.

Those passions are not required by the disciple of God. The passions required are true love, peace, and understanding. They may be gained in part by befriending an animal and raising its sensibilities above the animal level by sharing the warmth and kindness of beautiful human companionship with it but nothing can be gained by eating it. Therefore, as has been stated before, "thou shalt not kill". It is necessary for the student on the path to God to become a vegan so that he does not poison his physical form nor his bodies of light with the evil emanating from an animal that has had its life torn from it prior to its natural term. Nor is it acceptable to eat any by-products of an animal's death. Nor yet any fruit of that animal such as eggs, milk, or cheese.

To be a disciple, it is necessary to eat only fruit, nuts, raisins, vegetables, or pulses. Anyone who thinks that he may enter the kingdom of God and eat meat is deluding himself. God's kingdom deals in realities, not delusions. The Christ Jesus, it is noted in the Bible, ate from time to time fish, lamb, and various other meats and yet he was from God, of God, and returned to God. Why and how is this? If he were sufficiently enlightened, he should not have consumed the flesh of animals. Therefore, there appears to be a dilemma.

The answer 2000 years later is difficult to state with any certainty. Should Jesus have been born today, it is certain that he would have been a vegan. That can be stated a certainty because his views today are known to us. As to the past, it is probable that he ate meat. Perhaps there was nothing much else to sustain the body. Perhaps he ate meat in order to associate himself with those whom he taught and to those whom he offered enlightenment. Perhaps the Greek translation admitted to mention that he only ate vegetables. Perhaps, as the stories were transmitted by word of mouth throughout time, they became corrupted in the views of those who could not imagine that anyone could survive on vegetables alone.

We shall never know for certain and let it not be a stumbling block for the future. It is certain today that meat is harmful to man and will prevent him from obtaining the goal that he seeks. By being a vegan and by being a disciple of God, it shows others how to live and in the degree that others become vegans, then, hopefully, violence will decline in the world and peace will reign as it should. Therefore, those who would aspire to perfect physical health and those who would aspire to use that physical health as a means of directing their energies inwards and upwards to strengthen their bodies of light are required to observe diet as a spiritual act of obedience to God. Then that food ingested will not only replenish the physical form but will also generate streams of energy into the astral realms, strengthening and revitalising them with vibrant spiritual power which will enable those auras to act as vehicles of consciousness when the individual is ready and able so to do.

Discussing the role of diet in connection with the complexity of a total human condition leads one to pose certain pertinent questions. Those questions would relate to the effect of that diet upon the metabolism and would make considerations concerning the effectiveness of that diet in maintaining the metabolism in a working and balanced condition. Consideration would also be given to the effect that the diet would have upon the spiritual bodies of light for it is by no means just a one-way flow of energy that emanates from the bodies of light to the human form.

The process, as with so many others, is a dual one. Energy flows from the body to the auras. That energy is obtained initially from the food ingested and it is transformed and heightened in value according to the degree of spirituality of the individual and according to the original value of the food ingested. It may seem strange to consider that food of various sorts has potentially a varying capacity for spiritual manipulation according to the type of food that it is but it is so. The relationship between food and its spiritual value is complex but the potential value of any particular food may be altered by its suitability to the individual that is eating it.

Therefore, to give an example, the value of an animal may be considered to be greater than that of a plant. However, its potential for doing good is greatly affected by the conditions in which it was raised to adulthood, the manner in which it was treated on his trip to the slaughterhouse, and the manner in which it was killed. As has been previously mentioned, meat taken under those circumstances contains no benefit to humans and is actually harmful. The potential spiritual energy of such an animal is cancelled by the lethal auras emanating from its life and death, of fear and unhappiness, and that fear contaminates the meat, cancelling any potential for assisting humans to raise spiritual energy.

It has, in fact, the opposite effect. It lowers the spirituality of humans, thus, it was written earlier that it is not possible for a meat-eater to enter the kingdom of Heaven. No matter how strenuously an initiate strives to raise his consciousness towards the higher worlds, no matter in what degree he practices the techniques of meditation, etcetera, he is being dragged down below the level at which he started each time he ingests a mouthful of the flesh of an animal killed before its time set by God for it to die. Therefore, it is repeated that those who would aspire to reach towards God cannot successfully do so until all meat, fish, eggs, cheese, and dairy produce is eliminated from their diet.

By a similar process, one must consider another product that traditionally has been considered to be beneficial to mankind – honey. We will accept that everyone is familiar with the virtues of honey as a food and as a medication, but a similar process applies when it is ingested to that of when meat is taken. Because the bees are reluctant to give the honey away, it has to be stolen from them. Therefore, the stealer, the beekeeper, has sometimes to harm them with smoke in order to affect his crime and then he plunges the living embryo bees into boiling water to kill them to melt the wax and obtain his harvest.

The sensitive needs no further graphic portrayal of the aura attached to honey. With meats, one sin is performed – "thou shalt not kill". With honey, two crimes are committed – "thou shalt not kill" and "thou shalt not steal". So all are advised to omit honey from their diet as that too will prevent a person from entering the kingdom of Heaven should it be consumed. One is not permitted to become at one with God whilst one's life is full of sin and therefore it is necessary to become a true vegan should one desire to make at-one-ment one's goal.

Let us now consider the subject of which food it is possible to eat in order to derive the greatest possible benefit. First, it is necessary to state that no one should consume more than is necessary in order to maintain himself in health. Vegetables are alive and although it is considered necessary for humans to eat them in order to retain their health and their lives on Earth, it should also be remembered that those vegetables are harvested against their will and the same type of aura surrounds a vegetable taken against its will as would surround a piece of meat.

Fortunately, as the degree of sensitivity of vegetables is low, the amount of hatred, pain, and fear that they are able to generate is very little and so the benefits they donate to the human is greater than the harm generated by absorbing the aura of hate. But it must be realised that the more food that is taken, the greater the degree of hatred, etcetera, ingested. Therefore, it is advisable to eat only sufficient to maintain perfect health.

Next, it is necessary to broach the complex subject of which foods are safe for people to eat. As was hinted at earlier, that varies according to the rays along which people travel which corresponds to the signs of the zodiac. These rays are necessary for people and for animals and plants and, indeed, all life is generated and progresses by means of carrier waves of various types and frequencies. As to the reason why and how all this happens, the reader is referred to the appropriate chapter. At present, let us accept the validity of the rays, the signs of the zodiac, as applying not only to the human race but to all life in every aspect of manifestation.

Thus, we may see that by focusing on the vegetable kingdom and including nuts, fruits, and pulses, these too are split into groups and will be separated, one group from another, by virtue of differing waves. It may also be appreciated that those groups of vegetables of a particular ray would blend most suitably with a human of the same ray. Therefore, it is proposed to announce that for a person to comply with the pull of that wave which has carried him for many, many years so far, it would be better that he should begin to limit his diet to those foods which comply with his needs according to that ray.

*As I said at the beginning of this chapter, the actual list of food has been removed until it can be updated. Bob Sanders*

# CHAPTER 7 - AURAS

To describe in simple terms the action taking place within the aura of an individual as he or she performs any action would be, as is so often the case in spiritual matters, to simplify the facts to the point where reality would have no further meaning. In essence, the action of the power of God flowing throughout the auras of a sentient being is straightforward enough but the mechanics relating to and regulating that flow require deep analysis and study.

The auras contained within the life force that prescribes the parameters of a human being are several in number and various in hue. It is generally supposed that there are 7 distinct auras. It is not so. In essence, there is only one aura but that aura can be considered to form a number of distinct bands which relate to areas of emotion and intellect. However, a description of such auras would be incorrect if it was left to the understanding of the student that the major bands which constitute the vital elements of humanity are separate and distinct, one from another.

They are not. They are joined in one continuous octave of light and power, which responds and scintillates in response to the urge of intellect and soul. Action takes place in all areas of the aura and it is important to realise that humanity, indeed all life, is interrelated and joined via the higher elements of the aura, both in the sense of all sentient beings being connected and also in the realisation that oneness of life is the connection between man and God.

Therefore, let us assume that the connection between man and his God is resolved into the beauty of a relationship based on purity and love – surely, concepts of the highest quality that may never be sullied by interpretation or misrepresentation. The relationship can be of the highest but it is obtainable in the degree that the individual is able to bring his spirit to the fore in relationship with his ego and personality. Suppression of ego is ultimately necessary before such conditions may be made manifest as to elicit the required state of mind. Ego, whilst necessary for creation of identity whilst the soul sleeps, must and will reduce as soul growth is achieved. Thus, the power of wisdom will seem to gleam in the eye of an advanced soul instead of the glare of ego defending itself against an intruding nation.

Such states require great peace within the soul before success comes. How easy it would be if action brought results, if fighting achieved goals, and if power struggle achieved oneness with God. The opposite is true. Letting go of ego, of fear, of drive and ambition achieves success. Wisdom comes to those who have nothing to live for in a material and commercial sense, who will never be rich or famous in their time, and yet, such people live for everything, gain all, and their names are hallowed throughout the spiritual realms. Can it be that one detects a familiar ring to such concepts? Does it suggest, once again, that real life is at total variance to earthly existence? If so, why is this? God made the Earth and everything in it. As he created the spiritual realms, he created all life. Why then is the planet Earth the sole area where success based on measurement applicable to that plane is the opposite to success achieved in any other area?

The answer is both complex and simple. The simple truth is that it is necessary for most humans to experience heat and cold, pain and pleasure, success and failure, and all the emotions that are available on Earth. One must experience them in order to reject most of them and, in the process, to grow in stature. Could you sympathise with anybody in pain unless you yourself had experienced that pain? Could you appreciate the feelings of those suffering from hunger, thirst, heat, and cold unless you too had firsthand knowledge of those matters? So, you grow in stature when you appreciate the things of beauty and true pleasure, decide to seek those things of beauty and decide to bring them close to you. You grow also when you have the ability to inflict pain and unhappiness and decide not to. You grow as you help those suffering from the results of their own and other people's folly.

These things can only be experienced here on Earth. Such feelings as life on Earth generate can be echoed in other realms of existence and there are other planes where there are startling events waiting to be experienced. But this plane, Earth, provides the greatest degree of experience concentrated and concertinaed in time than any other plane. Experience it to the full if you will. Ultimately, whether you be the greatest sinner or the most glorious saint that ever trod the highways and byways, you will finish up at God's side.

It must be said that if you wish to be a criminal, a sadist, a pervert, or a murderer and you deprive yourself of those experiences through some reason other than the realisation of their incorrectness in relation to goodness, then it is possible that you may have to reincarnate in order to experience them at a later date. However, it is not suggested that such desires should be given free reign but it is suggested that imprisonment, unless it truly reforms the character of the miscreant, is not actually the answer to that individual's problem. It does, however, remove from society that individual, thus offering protection to the public.

It may be, of course, that such an individual, once he dies from Earth and goes to his new home in the spiritual realms, may find himself in an area where he can, at least mentally if not physically, subject those of similar nature to himself to the terrors that he would have done on Earth and be himself subjected to them until he realises that there must be better ways of existence and outgrows those concepts.

Therefore, it is plain that the planet Earth is of vital importance to the growth of immature souls and is the only area to provide such experience. It is also important to realise that we who tread on Earth do so because, initially, we sleep from a spiritual point of view and that it is our duty to awaken the soul. Then, and only then, can we rise above the limits of the Earth. Strange, then, that the individuals who have awakened their souls often exclude the possibility of the realities of greater life as are mentioned in this publication. Strange that such people who have the opportunity to experience the beauty of the greater realities still cling to the old, fear-ridden ways, and shut them out.

Still, as with all life on Earth, physical death brings release and once such individuals are able to appreciate the ongoingness of existence, they soon pick up the reigns and enter fully into spiritual life. We must appreciate, therefore, that the auras surrounding a living object, including humans, interpenetrate the auras of all other living things and also that they interpenetrate the physical regions of that living organism in the task that they accomplish.

Further, once something is touched by God, it can never die. All things that exist have been created by God and are, therefore, in a state of everlasting life. So the auras surrounding you also interpenetrate with the auras of every human, animal, plant, or mineral that was ever constructed by the hand of God and your auras interpenetrate with them. In that way, the past and the present are interrelated and we may say that time, as understood on Earth, does not exist. There is only sequence of events. The future does not conform to this pattern entirely although the near future relates to the present and is, in part, tied to it.

We wish to make it clear to you that, via the auras, you are part of every human that has ever lived, is living, or will live. Also, that you are part of everything from the largest planet to the smallest microcosm conceivable. All is one, one is all. There is only one and its name is God. You are part of the one. You are part of God but you are total God as you were created by God. Consider this concept. Meditate on it. It is a great truth, probably the most fundamental truth that you can begin to comprehend. You will not be able to prove the truth of these words until you have advanced to the point where you may operate in the auras. Then you will know that these words are true. In the meantime, accept, if you can, the value of this statement and allow it to become part of your reality. You will be taking a giant step in your progress.

Therefore, from the general, the concept of the greater outline of description of the auras, let us turn inwards to examine the particular, the several auras that man can see if he has the faculty and about which such interest is taken. There are, in fact, 7 distinct auras that may be appreciated by clairvoyant sight though, as stated before, the auras are not separate but interpenetrate one another in a glissando as compared to an arpeggio. The auras interpenetrate the human body at points which have been described in books on mystical matters since time immemorial, namely, the base of the spine, the spleen, the solar plexus, the heart, the throat, the brow, and the head.

These entry points are named chakras and form a connection point into the physical body so that information and life force may pass in a two-fold manner between the body and the auras. However, appreciate that the aura relating to any particular chakra is not merely a cloud of colour like a balloon attached to that individual. It is a body of fine matter seated within a planet of fine matter and able to connect or appreciate the reality of all similar life at that level. We add further that each chakra is a living, real, and active part of you, placed on a part of the planet of similar vibration to that aura, and able to appreciate the reality and value of life at that level which, in turn, has realities usually on the physical level.

Therefore, it may be appreciated that any particular aura has its base within an area of similar vibration to that aura, just as the physical body is placed within an environment of vibration that enables contact with that environment to be made *(Earth)*. An aura, so placed, must therefore, assuming that the body of the aura is sufficiently developed, be able to appreciate existence at that level and be at one with life at that level.

This process holds true for all of the auras that surround a living organism. Not only is the physical body placed on a physical Earth and able to make contact with everything on that physical Earth but each aura is similarly placed. Just as you may contact another human by speech – the process involving physical movement of air – by sight – the process involving physical particles of light – by smell, and by touch, at the same time, the auras of any two or more individuals are able to reach out and achieve a communication by etheric means at any level applicable to those individuals. Physical means of communication can, therefore, between any group or groups of individuals be superseded by auric communication.

Should this occur, the limitations placed on communication at an earthly level do not exist and one is able to contact those whom one wishes over vast distances and throughout time. Such means of communication is, however, limited to those who have developed the auras to the point where they are able to sustain the power and weight of the spirit. When an individual first incarnates onto the Earth, he is perforce born into the body of a baby. That baby is virtually unable to communicate in any meaningful fashion for a number of years. As time passes, the infant grows and, as he grows, so his ability to contact and express his thoughts and ideas becomes greater. Eventually, he matures to the point where he is at his greatest maturity.

It must be noted that the level of communication between any two individuals at the height of their intellectual maturity may differ widely. A moment's consideration of, for example, a bushman from Australia attempting to communicate meaningfully with a professor of an English university will suffice to appreciate that levels of communication between people differs widely and is in no way a measure of intelligence. However, to return to the concept of a baby growing to maturity, it should be appreciated that as the youth grows, so the ability to interact with his environment and with those surrounding him grows.

The auras of most individuals who incarnate on Earth are in a similar state to that of the newborn babe. Thus, interaction and communication, the flow of energy from and to the auras is at a minimum. This is because a) most people do not realise that they have auras, and therefore b) they make no effort to develop them and c) the development is tied to soul growth to a certain extent. Therefore, initially, and usually, most humans incarnating on Earth are tied to the experiences of the five Earth senses. All else remains unsavoured. However, through the now-familiar process of meditation, prayer, and devotion to God, the auras can quite quickly become developed, thus allowing interaction in a truly three-dimensional plane to occur. Should students of Godlike ways develop the aura sufficiently then true, instant and accurate communication may occur at will, without the need for speech at all.

The process whereby this book is conceived and transmitted follows that pattern. Members of The White Brotherhood, far removed from each other in terms of spiritual development, are able to join their minds into a consensus of opinion as to the quality of the information to be conveyed and then that information is implanted into the mind of the instrument on Earth who seeks to receive, accurately, that information. The process is one of merging of auras and of conveyance of information from one aura to another.

The process may be likened to that of a chain reaction where an event triggered at one end moves on until it is mirrored at the far end. At no time during the conveyance of information written here has the aura of the highest, most developed soul, actually touched the aura of the lowest soul but, nevertheless, the information has been passed from mind to mind until the desire of the group is achieved. This process is open to all who would accomplish the necessary growth. Should any individual achieve that growth, the strengthening of the auras, then he or she is free to reach out with their minds and experience the realities at any level into which they may reach.

Often, the only souls that they can reach are discarnate and, even then, they often tend to be guides and teachers, as few on Earth have the necessary soul growth to move within the auras and, even in the life after death, the majority of individuals are content to stay within their peer groups. Few venture into the voyages of discovery to be made by transferring consciousness into the auras. However, do not be dismayed. Should you make the effort to achieve the results mentioned above, you will have great freedom – freedom to observe the planes of beauty as well as the doleful places and freedom to contact elevated souls. So you will achieve soul growth as a move towards God that much quicker.

Could it be that one is able to contact beings of equal status in terms of development and that such contact would be meaningful? Should contact produce results gauged to enlarge upon the soul experience of the individual? It is that experience and interrelationship with other people often brings little direct reward. Not everybody is an advanced and pure soul – far from it. The vast majority of humanity incarnate on Earth and discarnate is entrapped still within the enfolds of materialism, for, do not suppose that lack of physical body brings release from materialistic and earthly desires – far from it.

There are large groups of beings who may have lived in the spiritual realms for long ages, measured by earthly standards, who have not loosed the bonds of desire. They satisfy those desires as best they can by creating with their minds areas of illusion within which they can conform to a standard of discipline and that area appears real to them. They accept that each of them plays a part within the illusion and each individual tends to accept his role and also the role of his contemporaries in maintaining a sense of realism. This concept may seem strange when it is realised that, by expanding vision, the illusion would disappear and freedom would obtain.

But the majority of people who inhabit the surface of the Earth conform exactly to this pattern. The illusions created by people since the dawns of humanity's earthly existence are carefully maintained by creating patterns of behaviour to which all must conform, laws being created to perpetrate the illusions, and those challenging the sense of normality being removed from society. Should one seek to change the pattern of reality clung to by the majority, the individual concerned is quickly exposed, his power effectively removed and the damage rapidly repaired. Do you believe this to be a true assessment of the civilisation within which you live?

We are taught not to think along expanded lines and we are encouraged and rewarded by society for maintaining established concepts and by working within them to strengthen them. Consider, for example, the reaction of establishment if it was proposed that orthodox religion is not necessary and that every individual may have a direct relationship with God and that there are no need of priests, representatives of God, of ceremony, of icons, and of ritual. Is it conceivable that people would be allowed, encouraged even, to sit where they are at home, at employment, in a park, and to meditate without attending Church, without having a religious body to direct their thoughts? Can you imagine a situation where all people throughout the world would lay down their weapons, where the armed forces disband, where barriers and frontiers between nations are ignored, where passports and visas are not sought, and people banded together in brotherhood? Can you imagine the reaction of establishment to those concepts?

And yet, the truth is, the reality is, that God is in all and everything. Mankind is one. There are no need of Churches, of dignitaries, of secret chambers and societies. There are no need of walls, of barriers, of exclusivism. They are illusions created by society and carefully maintained in order to preserve what? Illusion. It exists for its own sake and yet appears real. Soul growth destroys illusion. Therefore, Churches throughout the world, by and large, emasculate the soul and make people slaves to religion and not sons of God. The knowledge that all men are brothers would destroy the sense of separatism and so each race, each country, is seen to be a potential enemy to hide the truth and yet it is so patently obvious that the truth is true.

Leaders of religion throughout the world spout doctrines of peace and oneness with God and at the same time perpetrate the exclusivity of their particular brand of religion, ensuring that the simple souls who attend that Church fill their minds with false doctrines, thus perpetuating the illusion. It is law in many countries that a particular religion is taught in schools and, in some countries, it is law that the indigenous population conform to a Church. Whilst there are some benefits in conforming to apparent  norms, it does restrict soul growth of individuals, which is unforgivable. It puts off, indefinitely, the days of turmoil that must and will result from each individual's awakening into the light of truth.

Often, as was mentioned earlier, such an event is delayed for long ages even in the spiritual realms, for those who still conform to the normality applicable on Earth keep within their own group and seldom encounter an enlightened one. Thus, they reinforce the concept that their normality must be correct, the only way to be. Individuals do, however, awaken from time to time and they are helped upon the path to reality. We encourage you, in peace and in love, to challenge the concepts to which you conform. Do so in meditation. Ask yourself a question and allow the answer to fill your heart.

Seek to transcend the limits of your mind and gradually, as you expand your consciousness into the auras, you will feel the truth that those auras reveal to you. You will feel the oneness with God, the brotherhood of all mankind, your oneness with all life that exists. You will be able to explore the spiritual realms and know that they exist despite the mass of indignant people who pretend and hope that they do not. You will sense complete peace as you realise that there is nothing to fear, nothing unknown, no dark secrets withheld from you, that God is a God of love and peace and not the vengeful tyrant that He is portrayed in many books purporting to contain the true message. As you realise these facts, so you wonder why you spent so long in the land of Maya.

However, be warned. Those who control and are immersed within the grand illusion do not take lightly to looking upon someone standing in the light. They will hurt you with whatever means they have at their disposal. Many countries, now somewhat civilised and allowing certain freedoms, will limit themselves to verbal assault but, in some areas, the bringer of light will be put to death. It happened to Jesus over 2000 years ago and could still happen to you.

Therefore, the advice given is to follow your God as you can in peace and in quiet. Do not wear your newfound freedom on your sleeve. Jesus himself often encouraged people to whom he brought light not to tell anyone and the same applies today. Keep your own counsel. "Cast not pearls before swine or they will surely turn and bite you". Disseminate your newfound knowledge only to those who are seekers themselves and who will understand and grow in stature with you.

To continue to investigate the material from which the auras are composed and to follow the investigation as to why they exist and why they reflect colour, we need to comprehend the nature of matter. Scientists on the Earth have expended a great deal of energy and have made miraculous strides in investigation of physical particles. They have made the quantum leap of realising that matter exists outside of the realms that may be observed and measured by orthodox techniques. This is good because those investigators have begun to put aside telescopes and microscopes and have begun to work in the areas known as pure physics.

This involves the use of the mind instead of the senses and thus doors may be opened into realms which we call spiritual but to which most scientists ascribe a more pragmatic appellation. We do not wish to become bogged down by terminology. The point being made is that investigation can effectively and correctly be performed using that most powerful of instruments, namely, the mind. Mind is not brain. Mind does not calculate and quantify. Mind is. Mind reaches out into the areas of knowledge and receives information directly. Mind is at one with all that exists and is a part of the God concept. As such, it is only limited by the individual's entrapment within his body. Should he reach out, he may find.

Therefore, scientists working in pure physics are, at last, using the tool that they should have used all along. Their investigations have led to the suggestion that matter exists outside and beyond the atomic particles which constitute physical matter. Their investigation ought, ultimately, to reveal to them that matter exists on a number of planes, each separate, one from the other and yet each joined into a composite whole which includes the original particle that constitutes the atom that they commenced investigating.

This concept of matter relating to various planes was mentioned earlier in this chapter and is repeated now in order to take up and expand upon. It is made quite clear, then, that a piece of matter may exist on an earthly vibration and would constitute all that we observe around us on Earth and that same piece of matter also exists on a number of other realms of higher vibration, to use an expression readily understood, which has its basis of reality in a world visible and solid at each particular level. The same piece of matter is repeated several times and yet the totality of its several forms is one piece of matter.

Why should this be? The answer to this question will lead us into another area which is almost a subject for discussion in its own right and yet must be understood before the question posed can be answered. Matter is alive. Matter is life. Nothing exists that has not got solidity in one area of existence. Therefore, everything is alive and everything is real and solid, touchable and quantifiable. The essence of life is change. Nothing that is alive stays the same forever. The pattern of birth, growth, decline, and decomposition – death is an incorrect term as nothing can die – is universal. This pattern is vital to the ongoingness of existence.

Change is the only constant. If any single thing could remain unchanged forever, all life would cease as all life is one. A mayfly lives for a few hours and follows the pattern of birth, growth, decline, and decomposition. A solar system endures for countless millennia and yet, unless it followed the same pattern that applies to the mayfly, that beautiful creature could not have existed because it could not have followed its destiny of being born, of growing to maturity, of mating, of becoming feeble, of its life force being withdrawn, and of its body decomposing, the energy so released replenishing that used by the creature during its brief sojourn on Earth.

All is one. The solar system and the mayfly are one. They must conform to the same rules and therefore we may say that everything, including the solar system mentioned above, was born, grows, will decline, and will ultimately decay and will release matter to replenish that which it used whilst in its prime. This fourfold process is necessary because flexibility is the key to continuance. Change is an inbuilt requirement for living. Thus, as any creature or object exists, it is studied by an archangelic force that exists to control life and who are termed the directors of life and note being made of any shortcomings in that being studied so that improvements may be affected in the continuing strive towards perfection of that object.

Once change has been effected in that particular object or being, then, of course, change will be required in everything else to keep in balance the concept of all being one. That being the case, why do not the directors of life leave well alone and sit back to rest on their laurels? This is because change of circumstances relating to all that exist is constant. Time does not exist but sequence of events does and the moment now is not the same as the moment passed or the moment to come. As matter decays and is released following a natural law concerning balance of power, then the systematic following of events brings with it the possibility of corruption occurring.

This, in turn, is under the control of a force of beings whom we normally consider malign. They are not so. They exist to clean up the debris after anything has declined and are an essential part of life. They have their parallel on Earth. There are many creatures who exist to dispose of the waste of sentient life, who perform a vital role in maintaining a balanced environment where life can continue but they too have to be kept under control.

Similarly, in the area of life under discussion, the complement of the directors of life perform a vital function but they would perform it too well if the directors of life relaxed and thus they strive to pick up the pieces after something has declined and thrust it forward with suitable modifications. Therefore, we portray an existence where nothing is stationary. Even after the death of an object or creature, the essential logos, or concept, is pulled either towards perfection or towards decline. Gradually, matter is wrestled from the grasp of those archangels who work for decay and that matter is brought safely within the enfolds of the power of the directors of life.

Remember that matter refers not only to that in a physical sense but also in terms of the several layers that contribute to its totality. Once that matter is claimed then the opportunity exists for it to be manipulated and altered in concept in preparation for taking up a new role as a constituent part of some other live object. To illustrate the point, we might consider a plant, a daffodil, which, in the spring, thrusts upwards its leaves towards the light, flowers, fades, and then the leaves eventually will die back. The energy released by the death of the leaves is considered by gardeners to contribute to the growth of the bulb or root of that plant. It is said that the energy returns down the leaves and into the bulb again, the goodness nourishing that plant. The result is a growth of that particular bulb and, hopefully, birth of several more small bulbs, each destined to become fully-fledged daffodils in furtherance of that species of plants' continued existence.

However, the facts are slightly different than appears from a simple examination of the physical events. It is true that the leaves die back and it is also true that nutrients are returned into the bulb but, at different levels, other events are occurring. Whilst the process of decay of the leaves of a daffodil is occurring, the angelic forces charged with producing decay are hard at work causing a breakdown of the tissue of the leaves so causing nutrients to be released.

But, at the same time, more importantly from the daffodil's point of view, the directors of life are ensuring that the energy released in terms of the atoms that constitute physical nutrient is examined as regards the higher level of those atoms and, from those higher levels, slight changes to the genetic makeup are affected that will cause minute changes to occur within the format of the daffodil, in line with slight changes occurring on the planet Earth in terms of soil constituents, temperature, moisture, and also changes in the orbit of the Earth in relation to the sun. These genetic changes are designed to ensure that whatever conditions prevail on Earth, the plant will survive because it has been altered to fit its changing environment, a process known as adapting to change.

Thus, to make it clear, we will elucidate further by stating that during the process of decay of a leaf of the plant under discussion, the original atom in a physical sense becomes altered by changes being effected to its structure by manipulation of its auras. It is a fact that in the spiritual terms under consideration, the higher the vibration, the more easily may matter be manipulated and so the directors of life start at the top, at the aura of highest vibration, effect the required change, and then cause that change to be reflected in lower and lower auras until the physical atom becomes altered.

However, the process of change uses energy. That energy must be obtained from somewhere. There is only one source of energy in the universe and that is obtained from raised matter. As the vibration rate of matter is increased, so it emits energy rather like the process of blowing on a dully glowing ember of coal and causing it to glow more brightly. The change from dull-red to almost-white is mirrored by release of heat energy. This analogy is not scientifically correct and is used merely to illustrate the point and those who have immediately picked up the flaws in that description should not, therefore, suppose that the information being disseminated is also flawed. The concept of energy being released as the vibration rate is increased is true and is the backbone of continued existence by everything that was, is, and ever will be.

To return to the dying leaf, energy is drawn from the process by taking the logos, or concept of life, at a near-physical level and spiritualising that energy so as to transfer that logos into the next aura. The process is repeated until the logos – life force, call it what you will – reaches powerfully to the highest aura. This process, which amongst sentient beings is largely left to those beings, is effected by the directors of life. Once the life force has reached the highest aura, the changes mentioned above are caused and then the process of returning that life force down the auras and into the physical structure of the atom is effected, the atom now not being quite the same as it was when it began to be manipulated.

The energy released by the process of raising vibration is, of course, returned to the atom during the process of descent and balance is restored.

As was mentioned earlier, such change is designed to allow the plant the greatest possible opportunity to develop in an ever-changing environment to ensure the ongoingness of that plant. Of course, no one is perfect and sometimes changes wrought by the directors of life are not compatible with the environment that alters in unpredictable ways and so that particular plant, or group of plants, fails to survive. However, you must realise that the process of change is being wrought upon every plant all over the world and, so, many do survive. Some alter and become new species by a process gardeners call a "sport" which are changes occurring in the somewhat unpredictable manner as a result of the genetic engineering being wrought from on high.

Therefore, the auras surrounding that atom of a leaf, of a daffodil, will alter as vibration is raised or lowered and as energy is created or absorbed. The process occurs fairly slowly in a plant and so, to those of clairvoyant vision, little or no change would occur during any period of observation. Nevertheless, these changes do occur and could be examined by clairvoyant of sufficient talent, experience, and patience.

Great stock is taken of colours relating to the aura. One might question why auras have colour at all. The answer is quite simple in terms of acceptance of earthly colours. White light from the sun is composed of many individual colours. The reason why this is so will not be discussed at this point. Let us accept that white light may be observed to contain the colours of the rainbow and every other possible combination that the eye and the brain can quantify. It may be scientifically verified that white light is composed of a wide spectrum of vibrations and each band of vibrations corresponds to a colour. Thus, we know and accept that red is of a much lower rate of vibration than blue, blue being much higher in terms of vibration than red. The other colours fit in-between or expand above and below the blue and red according to their vibrancy rate.

It was stated earlier than an atom has a physical body and has 7 auras. The physical body of that atom is bathed with white light from the sun and, because it vibrates, it will respond in sympathy to the rate of vibration of a colour of the solar spectrum. The first aura of an atom has its reality in a world identical to that of Earth though removed in terms of a different set of vibrations. Therefore, the first aura will correspond to a colour commensurate to the vibrancy rate of light being emitted by that auric sun and so the process goes on.

Thus, each aura can be seen to glow a particular colour according to its vibrating rate. These colours may be termed the atom's base or quiescent colours. As energy is raised or lowered through the auras of that atom by the directors of life, so, of course, the auras would increase or decrease in vibration and would, therefore, change colour as they vibrate in sympathy with whatever band of the white light they are corresponding to in any particular auric solar system.

This image may be understood more readily should one consider a situation in which matter is caused to vibrate in sympathy with the magnetic field as is achieved in a microwave. Although in that case colour is not involved, the action of causing an object to raise its vibration rate releases energy in the form of heat. Should that energy be contained within a perfect vacuum, it would remain in the same state, hot, forever. However, nothing remains stationary. The perfect vacuum cannot be achieved in practice and therefore heat will slowly escape into the surrounding atmosphere until the object under consideration returns to ambient temperature. The heat released into the atmosphere would be equal to the energy used to create the magnetic field originally. Therefore, balance in terms of energy is maintained.

To return to a point that was discussed briefly earlier on in this study of the auras, we were considering what events were necessary in order to regulate the flow of energy through those force fields that constitute auric growth. It is in the interest of the student to try to comprehend the nature of life. It is considered by those incarnate on Earth and who are sufficiently tied to it not to realise the magnificence of God's only creation that life is connected with an object's electrical field and that may be seen to stimulate nerves of a sentient creature and follows the outline of a plant. But, just as the mystery of what is God could not be answered, similarly, life is a concept that equates with God and will remain unquantifiable.

Those of you who have followed the course of certain individuals, growing cultures, cloning creatures, and perhaps fooling themselves that they were getting closer to solving the mystery will be disillusioned. The creation of life is not within the gift of man nor yet is the answer to where and how life is created known to any person living in the higher realms of light. Certainly, it seems that the angelic forces that work for the power of God handle and manipulate life once it is created but, as to the origin of the creation of life, we merely accept that it is. We, too, like to investigate and we have a number of theories as to how life originates but, because we do not know for certain, we refrain from speculation.

Like you, we accept that we are alive and we know that we will live for as long as it is possible to imagine. We also know that the destiny of all life is to merge with the Godhead so that the circle of life can continue but we cannot describe the nature of life. We cannot give you the formula for making it. We cannot cut up a body and remove that life organ as we might with the liver, spleen, or heart. Similarly, and tied to the concept of life, is the soul. The soul is not the spirit of God within man. It is a vehicle. It is the vehicle that contains the essence of life rather like the shell of an egg contains the essence of a chicken. The soul will always remain in conjunction with the life force, protecting it and keeping it intact at least until the pair, soul and life force, merge with God. After that, we lose track of it and so we cannot comment.

However, we wish you to realise that in association with you and all your various auras, you have a final essence, the life force, and that life force is and will remain within that object called the soul. However, the soul has no special power and is not to be venerated. It is no more than a protective coating round a nut. The life force, which is both part of and the totality of the spirit of God, is that which should be venerated because it is God himself. The soul, of course, occupies no space and therefore is not actually within you. It is associated with you and is an essential part of you but is, in terms of vibration, even above the highest aura. Your soul is, because it is of God and God is all and one, unique and separate from every other soul and yet, at the same time, is one and part of every soul that is.

If you cannot grasp that concept intuitively, do not try to analyse it intellectually. You will not grasp the concept. You will grow to accept the truth as you grow in soul growth. Therefore, it is clear that, as all is one and all is God and all is alive, therefore, everything has a life force and, equally, everything has a soul. Do not accept Christian doctrines that plants and animals do not have a soul. It is false doctrine stated by those who should know better. Realise that, as you interrelate with plants, animals, indeed, rocks, sand, water, and everything that is, that it is all alive, it all has a soul, and that life force and soul is at one with you, separated from your mind only by your and its ego and personality.

Think of this should you eat an animal, kill a fly, and hack down a weed. They are not lesser than you. They are exactly equal to you and are indeed you. Treat all life as you would wish that life would treat you because, if you should deliberately harm anything, you are harming yourself. On the subject relating to consummation of food for health and to maintain your body, refer to the chapter on diet.

Having attempted to quantify, at least to some extent, that mysterious life force, we now turn to examine how that force relates to the human body. Mention was made earlier of a daffodil and attempts made to indicate that each atom of the plant exists in more areas than just the physical and that the totality of its physical and auric reality were one. We stop in our examination of atoms at this point because, in reality, we are not portraying the exact truth. We feel obliged to present the information about a point of life and how it exists and use the term atom to represent points of life.

In fact, atoms do not exist as rounded, solid objects and, therefore, we are using them as an example rather than portraying truth. We feel that if we tried to present to you the facts concerning singular points of life a) you would possibly not comprehend, and b) we would upset the balance of scientific knowledge by bypassing the long years that science has yet to take to relate to the truth. Also, it must be said that such concepts, as are alluded to, are capable of misuse as has been the atom and we do not wish to add to man's arsenal of destruction.

So, to repeat, there is a life force that runs throughout the total concept of each individual point of life which we will still refer to as atoms. At some point, a single atom has to decide whether it is going to form a drop of water, a piece of rock, a plant, an animal, or a human, and so we will consider why it is that the atoms that constitute a human do so instead of constituting a rock. If, in essence, it is true that every individual concept of life, which may be considered to be at the centre of every atom, originates from God, is the same and is one, it follows that, in essence, there is no difference between you and a piece of stone and yet clearly that is not so. You are a much more advanced form of life than the stone and will always remain so.

What is it that makes the difference? Certainly not God. God creates but he does not differentiate. He does not predispose certain points of life force with greater sentience than others. He creates all equally. Therefore, at some point, a singular life force must be directed to become a human and another must be chosen to become a rock. There are directors of life mentioned previously, an archangelic force who themselves are not human and could not be imagined by humans, who take the differentiated life forces and direct them to become what is needed, rather like a farmer might have a stream and direct it first it into one field and then into another as irrigation was required.

It is a rather sobering thought that the life force, which is the essence of you and which so many humans consider elevates him to greater importance, could so easily have been used to make a dog or a pig, a geranium or a cabbage, a stone or a raindrop. If this opens your eyes to the fact that you are no more important than a raindrop, then you will have learned a valuable lesson. However, human you are as you were created and human you are destined to remain. With it come certain obligations in terms of the raising or spiritualising of matter to further the ongoingness of life and therefore much effort is being, has been, and will be expended to assist you in realising the soul growth necessary to achieve that raised power.

Once the directors of life have located a deficit in any particular area – and we branch off once again to suggest that there are areas of life far beyond the planet Earth and far beyond the ken of even the most knowledgeable of you – they reach into that bank of life and release a certain amount of it. Let us suppose that it is decided to create humans. The life force drawn from the bank is then prepared in the required fashion. It would be placed within the force field called the soul and energies would be directed at it which would give it certain characteristics.

We do not describe these energies because it is not possible so to do. One cannot describe gravity, electricity, or the power of love. One can only describe their effects. Electricity is often quantified as "that force that" ... Such description tells one of its effects but ignores completely the nature of the force itself. Therefore, we will not try to pull the wool over your eyes except to say that a life force may be imbued with "that force that gives the life force human characteristics". We hope that you will appreciate the dilemma that such a hopeless description places us in.

We feel a burning desire to be open and honest with you but, in such areas, language does not exist to quantify such concepts. We merely ask you to accept that such forces exist which can and do give definition to differentiated life force.

Once this has been achieved, of course, the life force may be considered to be an embryo human. However, it consists of its life force, its soul, its human stamp, and nothing else. So begins the long process of movement down from the elevated plane in which the embryo was created onto a lower plane. That first lower plane would be the highest or seventh plane to which humans later ascend. In order to reach that plane and relate to it, a force field is pulled round the soul by a process akin to gravity and that soul now has an aura around it. That aura is, like the soul itself, merely a vehicle that enables the spirit of God to relate to the seventh plane, rather like a body enables you to relate to the Earth.

Later, the life force with its soul and seventh aura begins to descend to the sixth plane. As it approaches it, so another aura of the sixth plane merges and now the life force can relate to life on that planet. This process goes on until that life force merges with the human body at the moment of birth and we say that a baby is born. The human body is, of course, merely an aura when considered in the light of the above information, just as the auras may be considered to be bodies when viewed from the point of view of an earthly concept.

Once the point is reached that results in a baby being born, of course, the nadir or low point is reached in terms of descent and it is up to the individual to begin to spiritualise himself in order, in effect, to do the work that in the plant and mineral kingdoms is achieved by the directors of life, namely to spiritualise or raise energy back upwards through the auras until a state is reached where one has filled each aura with raised power. The subject of the effects and details pertaining to raised power at each stage, or aura, will be dealt with in due course.

We wish to make it clear to you that you are in effect on a cyclical course. You originated from God at the highest point conceivable, you descended into manhood, and now you are struggling to raise yourself back to the point where you started. Does this seem pointless? Well, it does and is pointless if you expect life to contain some great importance as regard yourself or if you imagined that you and your fellow men are in some manner divine above and beyond the divinity within any inanimate object. We are sorry to disillusion you. You are extremely important in one sense and one sense only.

You are part of a cycle of raising power, rather like being part of a stream being used to turn a water wheel. The water wheel represents the ongoingness of all existence and the stream represents all life. All life plays a vital part in raising energy and you merely act in a higher, more powerful sense than a raindrop. But, essentially, the need of a human being and a raindrop in God's plan are of equal importance. It is an essential part of the master plan. But, do not be dismayed. Having perhaps destroyed any delusion of grandeur that you may have been accustomed to through absorbing the teachings of orthodox religions, and perpetrated by those who wish to exploit nature for their own greed, we now wish to reassure you that, being human, you are indeed the chosen ones of God.

As was mentioned earlier, the differentiated life force is made into anything that requires to be manufactured by the directors of life and it is pure chance that you were made into a human. Having been selected by chance, you are now destined to lead an existence beyond your wildest imagination. Do not suppose that the drab world that you inhabit presently is indicative of all of creation. It is not. It's like living in a vast, most beautiful palace and you have merely seen the coal store. When you have climbed the stairway to freedom, you will be qualified to leave that black area and to visit and stay in the vast marbled halls which constitute the bulk of the palace.

However, we speak metaphorically of course. There are no palaces, no rooms in real life, but there is something much better. There are states of bliss that transcend your wildest euphoric states imaginable and the states of bliss are piled one on top of another in never-ending form, each one infinitely more exhilarating than the previous. The key to reaching those states is to follow the precepts given in this publication and to allow the power of God to fill all your auras, all your realities, driving out any base, fear-ridden concepts. You do not have to believe this to be true. Try meditation. Try devotion to God. Try prayer. Try to follow the advice given and you will see for yourself that it is all true and more. There is no limit to the joy that you can experience, only the limit that you place upon yourself.

Should you find that all this is beyond you, then do not feel guilty. Until you are ready, you cannot make the adjustment but we beg you – once you are ready to ascend the stairway to freedom, to life, do not remain in the coal cellar under the illusion that it is safe and comfortable, warm and friendly, and because those who are your leaders are there. Should any of your leaders, elders, and self-appointed betters stop the roundabout of illusion upon which they ride for one instant and visualise the brighter area waiting above them, they would abandon you in a moment. They ride the roundabout alone and in isolation, and they feel no brotherliness towards you. They merely use you for the benefit of their own egos and would leave you to dwell alone without a second thought if they had the chance to better themselves.

You too walk in isolation and although you feel the desire for togetherness, you will not find it in their company. True brotherly love awaits on the higher planes and you have a much greater chance of rising to those planes than those to whom you currently bow down. Leave them to be masters of nothing. The slaves may be free and may cross the River Jordan. Leave the Egyptians in the cellar to rant and rave, to make their plans exploiting themselves alone. You do not need them, they need you but you deserve a better master. Make God your master and serve only him. Then you can live in the land of Canaan in peace and in harmony with yourself and with all life.

Do not believe we are telling you the truth. Try it for yourself and we promise that you will realise that it is all true. Who knows? Perhaps, by your example, politicians, leaders of Churches, leaders of trades unions, and all those who now exploit the masses will realise the error of their ways and may turn in prayer to God and, instead of exhorting the masses to be slaves to their own half-baked theories, they may begin to loose the shackles so that individuals may too cross the divide between slavery and freedom.

You will have noticed, of course, that we used the story of Moses to illustrate the point that we made above. There are many, many stories in the Bible and none of them actually refer to historic events. They are all cleverly encoded accounts of your relationship with God and with your fellow man. The chosen people, the Israelites, are liberated souls, not just of the Hebrew faith but of all faiths and all of races and of all situations. The Egyptians are not the people of that country but represent all who enslave the minds and hearts of free men wherever they are situated.

It may come as a shock to anybody of the Jewish faith to realise that they are not God's chosen people but that is the fault of the rabbis who should have reached beyond the limits of the Torah and looked into their own souls to find truth. They should have known that God creates all men equal. You make yourself a chosen one by aligning yourself with God. It is in your hands and your hands alone. Thus it is that God may be found on a mountain top or in a prison dungeon. There are no bars to keep God from your heart and it is unforgivably criminal of anyone who has an inkling of the truth concerning God to keep it from the public through financial, theological, or political reasons.

The truth concerning God must and will be made available to all men, not the garbled stereotyped image perpetrated by most books and by most servants of Churches but the glorious freedom experienced in the hearts of those who seek instead of believing intellectually, who know through personal experience instead of acquired second-hand knowledge. Then may the world begin to be set to rights. Then may peace begin. Then may the prince of peace truly sit on his throne in the kingdom of God. We ask you in peace and in love to join that throng marching through the wilderness to freedom. It is your ultimate destiny. Do not put it off for one more day. You may have all of eternity before you but, oh, how precious is each moment, how beautiful, and how vital the course that we ask you to follow. Think on these words and, if you doubt them, pray for guidance. If you accept them, join us.

We ask, however, that if and when you do join us, you do so completely. There is no room for a part-time saviour. Allow yourself plenty of time to adjust to your lifestyle but, ultimately, we require you to follow the instructions contained within this book to the letter. We also ask you to act sensibly. We do not require you to change your lifestyle. We do not ask you to give up your employment nor to retire to a monastery. We ask you to adjust within, to live in peace with all men, to follow the diet applicable to your birth sign as far as is correct for you, but we do warn you to consult a doctor if you have any doubts about your health, and to consider diet as part of a routine of devotion to God.

We ask you to be considerate to all life, to pray, to meditate, and to analyse yourself daily. We also require you to respect your own intellect, which may be powerful or weak. Some can accept a life of prayer and rise to greatness on it.

Others of weaker intellect become "cranks". We do not wish any of you to practice any austerities. We do not require you to walk about with "the end is nigh" boards on your body. We specifically forbid you to mutilate yourself or to reach a point where you consider suicide as a means of reaching the other side. We specifically forbid you from harming any person, creature, or thing that refuses to conform to your newfound salvation. In short, should you be of a somewhat weak-willed nature, we would prefer that you do not attempt to follow the path to salvation with any great vigour. You have all of eternity in front of you and, eventually, you will mature to the point where you are strong and can take up the reigns and be a leader amongst men.

Further, we make one final admonition. As you develop spiritually, you will develop the gifts of the spirit. You will achieve powers that should be used for the benefit of mankind. However, just as electricity can be used to provide the motive power behind a heart pace-making machine or to energise an electric chair used in some prisons, so the raised power behind the gifts of the spirit are susceptible to misuse. There is great temptation, initially, to use your powers to smooth your daily round, to provide those things that karma has not provided you with, and to bring you amusement. Do not be so tempted. You will incur great penalty and could have the gifts removed from you.

Jesus, when confronted by Pontius Pilate, mentioned that he could have used his powers to save himself from the fate that awaited him but he realised that he was obliged to tread that path. Follow the example of Jesus. Use your powers to help others and you will be blessed by God. Reject any thoughts of using that power for self-help or for evil.

The study of the auras, as was mentioned at the beginning, is long and complex. The auras, which constitute a part of everything, thus interrelate with God and with the most base concept imaginable. Therefore, the auras are an integral part of all that is. As such, in fact, no book on esoteric matters would be complete without such study and also a study of the auras is all that is necessary to quantify knowledge on esoteric matters. As such, it must be appreciated that the degree of depth obtained by these few pages  will not afford any comprehensive study to be made and it is proposed, at a later date, that a thick volume be produced which will provide a consensus of all the knowledge that is currently available concerning the auras.

Naturally, such a book will in itself be a complete[primer of spiritual knowledge, but its slant will be from the point of view of the auras. Therefore, we wish to make it quite clear to the student that we have merely touched upon the subject, that sufficient information has been made available for the student to appreciate his relationship with God and with all life, and that we will complete the task of bringing enlightenment to the people of this world by compiling the volume mentioned above.

We hope, should you feel the need, that you will make the effort of reading this new proposed book and that it will create an even firmer base to your foundation of spirituality. We ask you to attune yourself always to the power of God flowing through the auras and to appreciate the immensity of that power.

# CHAPTER 8 - ORGANISATION OF DAILY ROUTINE

We are accustomed, within whatever society we happen to reside, to regard ourselves as being fairly at one with that society. We obey laws and conventions that enable us to fit into routines and follow codes of conduct that have an effect of enabling the society within which we live effectively to operate. This cohesion of different peoples with different backgrounds in terms of upbringing, education, class, and skills into one force is considered to be a vital and necessary manner in which society operates. Without such patterns of modification of behavioural manners, it is expected that society, as we know it, would crumble, that business life could not effectively be conducted, and that breakdown in general terms of law and order would ensue.

Certainly, we have a sort of balance maintained in terms of social, business, and political life and it is true that it is considered necessary to eject from society those who do not fit in and yet how much regard is placed upon the true quality of that life? How much consideration is apportioned by any living individual or group to the values that we acclaim to appreciate so much? We all respect law and order. Law and order, if you consider for a moment, point one in the direction of the concept called God. The originator of natural laws, the laws of nature, is God. The concepts of peace, love, and harmony are godly concepts. Order, the opposite of chaos, is the essence of the power of God. The coming together of matter, of life, of society in a cohesive, peaceful, and constructive manner is a God-like quality. Therefore, we must accept that law and order are rules that should impel the followers along a path designed to bring them closer to God.

However, how many people who use the law in their daily lives ever consider whether they are acting in a God-like manner? How many politicians, solicitors, judges, and business people who use the rule of law, who consult books of law, and who use the law to their own advantage realise that they are acting in contradiction to the concept of God? The contradiction, the opposite of God, is of course Devil. We work either for God or we are used by the forces of destruction. There is never any intermediate state. You must be aware at all times that because nothing is ever stationery, that change is the only constant, that you work actively for the power of good, or you will be used by the power of evil.

Do not suppose that you have to practice black magic in order to work for the dark forces. Do not suppose either that you are accused of being evil yourself. Very few people actually practice the black arts but many, many people are insensitive to the knowledge of the needs to strive actively for God. Many people still sleep in a spiritual sense and would, therefore, almost certainly fall prey to the power of evil. Therefore, we ask you to accept that, unless you study your motives carefully each and every moment of the day and act only in a way that you feel and hope will be of benefit to your fellow man, you will be used by the power of chaos and will bring unhappiness into your life, the lives of others, and will strengthen the grip that the devil has on the world.

Ignorance is no defence. The law works quite automatically for good or for evil and you work either for good or for evil. So next time you consider using the word "law" either in the sense of being law-abiding or by using man's laws to affect something, stop and reflect that only God makes laws and those laws, when reflected through you, should always bring peace, love, and harmony and happiness to all. Any other use of any type of law would bring you into the army of the lord of chaos. Choose and choose wisely.

We now turn to an aspect of the disciplines for obtaining peace and tranquility and consider the effect of pride. When man is born, he incarnates with an aura associated with him that is an essential part of him and is there to allow the life forces from his bodies of light access in a two-way manner between the physical body and those auras. This aura under discussion acts as a go-between, a staging post, for the essential spiritual forces that must interplay with man. It is extremely dense compared to the true auras and, although it has no life in itself, it is often animated by the spirit residing within it. It is called the etheric double. It is easy to see with the trained naked eye and appears as a white mist close to, but not touching, the body. Its sole function is to allow access to the human form and vice versa.

However, it often acts in a strange manner. Because it is both very close to the Earth in vibrational terms and because it is yet an aura, it is subject to influence by earthly emotional forces. These are given out by animals, by people both incarnate and discarnate. Its closeness to the Earth indicates that it does not have the benefit of influence by higher elevated souls. The only influence it receives is from crass, egotistical, and base forces. Therefore, it responds to those forces, vibrates in harmony with them, and as a result feeds those very negative attributes into the personality of the individual.

We usually find that a baby is very selfish, egotistical, and self-centred, etcetera. We accept that babies are like that and assume that it is a natural part of being a baby. It isn't. Babies born on Earth are able to accept information from all of their auras as can anybody else and, should that be the case, the infant would be loving, kind, and peaceful. However, because that child has not learned to ignore the pull of that etheric double, he is held within its grip and becomes the rather unpleasant creature that we all know. Fortunately, most of them, as they grow older, learn automatically to ignore information from the etheric double and begin to receive information from their true auras and thus they become more lovable.

We say that they grow out of those conditions but, of course, there are always exceptions. Some babies grow to manhood and are still held, at least to some extent, within the grip of the influence of the etheric double, thus feeding into their realities the base earthly concepts mentioned above. Such people are not very nice. They act quite impulsively and often violently. They have little or no control of their tempers. We call them childish, an accurate description for that is what they are. There is no correlation between the actions of an individual being influenced by the emotions transmitted to him through the auras and the action taking place within someone under influence of the malign forces.

In one, the auras accept a vibration of a particular rate or level and cause sympathetic vibrations to be set up within that individual and, in the other case, that of someone held in the grip of evil, the process occurring is one in which the action of the auras is being reduced through negative influence. Effectively, one process is the opposite of the other. However, the effect observed by another of the result of each type of interference often appears similar. Actions performed can be outbursts of violent temper or physical violence. The individual may fluctuate between bursts of good humour and deep despair, or indeed of outbursts against any individual with whom he may be in contact. But, the key to study of any person's behavioural patterns is to compare the actions of that individual to a known norm.

We do not understand how a person influenced by the devil might act but we are familiar with the actions of a child and we can compare the action of someone with that concept. Therefore, we assume that those who act in a typically childish manner would be still influenced by their etheric double. Those actions might well be, as was mentioned above, quick and violent outbursts of temper, selfishness, mindless cruelty, disregard for others, and possibly, the need for much sleep also as lots of nervous energy is used and is not replaced through the auras.

It is fairly easy to spot those trends within an individual including oneself. The appropriate action must, of course, be to allow the auras to expand through the trinity of prayer, meditation, and devotion to God. Slowly, the etheric double will reduce in importance as the auras fill with spiritual energy and balance is restored to that person. If one discounts childish behaviour, then all the negative trends within people must, to a certain extent, be the result of or credited to the dark forces. The other disagreeable states might include slyness, deviousness, excessive pride, the desire to succeed at the expense, if necessary, of others.

Perhaps the easiest way to comprehend the difference between the two states is always to bear in mind that children act in selfish yet harmless fashions. If their actions harm another, it is not by design but by accident. In the state of someone held in the grip of evil, the opposite applies. The essence of evil is that it should harm as many as possible. Thus, the person effectively influenced by evil would, by his desire to achieve success or fame, be quite at home with the idea of manipulating individuals or masses in order to gain his own ends.

We see the result in capitalism, or indeed communism, in their worst forms where groups of people are exploited for the benefit of one or more individuals. This is truly evil. It has resulted in the doleful lives of millions of people, who throughout time have been treated as slaves, as objects to be used and discarded when their use has finished. It has resulted in the wars that have rocked this planet since man first became aware of how to invent weapons and it directly results in much of the climatic upset that devastates large tracts of the world from time to time. It must be clear, then, that of the two types of behaviour under consideration, the second is by far the worst and should be eradicated from the auras as soon as possible.

From that, we turn to the concept of organisation of daily routine that will enable those wishing to follow the path the means of so doing. Routine must be established that will give the individual time to follow his employment and his worldly duties whilst, at the same time, will enable him time to retire in prayer and meditation and to the greater concepts of life so that he might enlarge the power within his auras, thus bringing peace and contentment to himself and with those with whom he comes in contact and will ultimately cause peace to reign in the world.

The first aspect that must be considered relates to rest. It is easy to fill one's life with activity, to drive oneself to the limits chasing a concept, pursuing an objective, but it must be realised that that is not the way to find peace within oneself. The first requirement is to care for the temple of the soul which is the body. That temple must be nourished adequately and sensibly and also sufficient rest must be taken to ensure that the body each day is renewed, regenerated.

How often do we wake in the morning and find ourselves exhausted following a night spent tossing and turning as our minds relived events of the day and events to come thus preventing us from wakening refreshed? It is important, therefore, that one realises that, before retiring each night, a state of mind should be entered into in which the day's events are dismissed, put behind one, so that deep and sound sleep may obtain throughout the night. Only then can one awaken sufficiently refreshed so as to face the day and sufficiently full of energy so as to complete the tasks that one has set oneself in pursuit of God.

It is therefore suggested that the student, before retiring, should sit quietly for a few moments and mull over the events of the day, make a mental note of that which has been left unfinished, and make a mental note of that which has been finished. Finally, one should place all of it in God's hands, pray for peace, and pray for rest, and no matter how little one has accomplished that day, how large the burden, one should attempt to put them upon one side in order to retire into deep and restful sleep.

With practice, that state may obtain. Like all things, the more one practices, the easier it becomes. If, as do so many, you are in the habit of reliving through dreams the events of the day, then you will need to break that habit and so it will take time. But, we urge you to persevere and, ultimately, you will begin to sleep the deep sleep of the just as you place yourself in God's hands, and thus gradually, as you awaken each day refreshed, energised, and able to face each day fully, you will achieve more and more. Then you will find that you are able to rest more completely each evening in the sense that you have completed each day the tasks that you set yourself.

Once awakened, it is suggested that, before rising, one says a prayer of welcoming to God and of placing oneself in God's hands for the day. Then, if one has sufficient time, it might be advisable to rise and, before commencing employment, to meditate for a few moments. However, that is not always possible. Therefore, should that not be possible, we suggest that you at least try to hold on to the concepts of peace and love and service to mankind as you travel to your employment, ignoring all the upsets that you see and hear and are party to upon your journey. Arrive at your employment, if you can, in a state of peace and tranquility and attempt to maintain that state throughout the day, involving yourself fully in the finer concepts that your employment entails but avoiding completely the base and negative aspects such as argument, jealousy, and seeking to advance oneself above one's fellow man.

If you keep your peace within yourself, you should arrive home in the evening still with sufficient energy to pass the evening without feeling exhausted. All too often, people arrive home from work embittered by the trials and tribulations of the day, feeling exhausted by the malign forces that have swayed around them, draining their psychic energies and leaving them feeling sick and tired. Should that happen to you, we suggest that, before you arrive at your work, you ask God to protect you, that you place a barrier of love around you mentally like a large umbrella and that you ensure that you do not break out from under that umbrella by entering into the arguments that your colleagues may try to involve you with. Keep your peace. Do your work. Serve your fellow man, but do not become involved emotionally with any backbiting or negative aspects that you may find, all too frequently, you have in the past been involved with. So it is hoped that you will learn to arrive home and still be feeling fit and well.

When you have completed your household duties and other things that you may have to do each evening, it is suggested that you sit and meditate for a period of time. The technique has been mentioned elsewhere and will not be repeated now but we suggest that prayer and meditation will advance you greatly. Thus, having meditated, it is suggested that, if you can, you pass the evening in quiet and in tranquility, perhaps reading, perhaps watching television if you wish, but we urge you not to become too involved emotionally with the films of violence that you see. Do not become involved with the newscasts showing violence and all the negative aspects which man glorifies so much. Then, as was mentioned earlier, we ask that you think about the day and then dismiss it and retire to bed to sleep the sleep of the just once again. Thus it is possible to fill your life with tranquility.

Should you do so, you will find that you are full of energy that, in the degree that you serve your fellow man in the correct fashion, God will send a vital force to energise you and you will be able to go on and on. However, as was mentioned earlier, there is a place for all things. There is a time for work and a time for rest and there is a time for sleep. In the Bible, it was considered that 8 hours work, 8 hours rest, and 8 hours sleep were the correct proportions. It may be so, it is up to you. You decide for yourself how much work you can do, how much rest you need, and how much sleep you need, but we ask that you respect that trinity, that you do not try and work all day and snatch a few hours' sleep. Neither do we ask that you spend your time in idleness achieving nothing. We ask that you try to strike a balance within your life of serving man, of drawing energy within yourself through the process of rest which should include meditation, and then that you finally recharge your batteries through beautiful sleep.

It is expected that by following this process, your health will improve, that your standing within the community might improve, and that you will become a centre for spiritual guidance for those who feel lost. Should that happen so that people come to you to discover the secret of your newfound health and vitality, we ask that you transmit the information to them in full as we have given it to you. By so doing, the word of God will be spread among the people of the world and the concept of peace, so vitally necessary today, will be spread as all mankind begins to relax, bathed in the beauty of the light of God shining from their souls.

Gradually, peace will be restored to individuals and to groups and to nations. First must come establishing the correct manner of living. No amount of hope, work, or argument will cause peace within the heart. No degree of passing of legislation, of creating armed forces, and of making weapons will bring the desired effect. The premier requirement is for each and every individual to establish within himself a code of conduct and ethic or behaviour that will bring peace and health into this heart and body. Then, and only then, can prayer and meditation be truly effective in strengthening the peace and the power within that individual.

From that platform may others be bathed in the golden glow of the power of God emanating from such an individual, thus causing within the souls of all lost and malcontent the first stirrings as their souls respond in harmony to the vibrant wave of power. Once stirred into life, the soul never sleeps again. So, we may assume that all who come into contact with a vibrant being are, to some extent, affected. They will have their souls awakened and thus they will be on the path to perfection whether they realise it or not. Their actions will diminish in terms of violence and anti-social behaviour.

We therefore look expectantly forward to the day when any individual with soul still sleeping cannot avoid but meet with vibrant-souled individuals wherever he may turn as the word of how, and why, to achieve spirituality is absorbed into beings of more and more people. This chain reaction must and will take place but it starts with you. Having been privileged by whatever means God chose to give you access to the information and directions of both the need for and the wherewithal how to achieve soul growth, you have a burden placed upon you to fill your existence with that soul growth until you become a light shining before the Lord.

Then, you too will influence others by bringing that light into their world, lighting their darkness. See to it that you do indeed become a shining example. Your future depends upon it. The future ultimately of millions of others depends upon it. The peace of the world depends upon it. Understand, if you can, the enormity of the responsibility we place upon your shoulders. We do not give you more than you can bear but we give you the maximum that you can carry. As you grow in stature, the burden will increase until you can carry the weight of the world on your shoulders as does Jesus. Like him, accept the load and put in your maximum effort for the rest of your days. Your reward will be beyond your wildest imagination as you reach the elevated heights of the masters.

As you begin to pray, to meditate, and to serve God in man, animals, plants, and all that exists, you automatically place yourself on the list for selection by the masters as a neophyte, or student. Over the months and years that you follow the trinity of prayer, devotion, and service to God, you will develop the gifts of the spirit. These may scarcely be noticeable to you or they may greatly develop as some so-called mediums have them in clairaudience - the ability to hear discarnate voices, clairvoyance - the faculty of seeing into different realms, clairsentience - feeling through the auras, the healing touch, and many other facilities.

As you develop the gifts, so the teachers and master who dedicate themselves to spreading peace throughout the world will begin to use you in various ways. You may indeed become a medium, spreading the word of the greater truths to people, or you may become a healer. Yet again, you may be required to preach, to write, or to communicate in some fashion the truth to mankind. By doing so diligently, you will be accepted more and more into the brotherhood and you will have yet greater tasks placed upon you. Ensure then that you complete each task that you are given to the best of your ability because only maximum effort is satisfactory to God. He will understand your limitations and failures but He sees also sloth and idleness.

Do not let that criticism apply to you. Seek always to maintain good health. Seek always to enjoy exercise and rest in the correct proportions. Nourish your soul with happy, harmless pursuits and hobbies, and you will be in a position to become a faithful servant of God.

Mention was made earlier of medium-ship. There are some people who call themselves spiritualistic mediums. The ability to develop the gifts of the spirit is open to all. It is a process that commences with meditation and finishes as the auras are developed thus enabling the individual to explore the realms relevant to the auras developed. However, as was mentioned many times, you have a number of auras. At their lowest level, they are little removed from the state of vibration of the Earth and, at their highest, are close to God. The stumbling block to developing the auras is soul growth, which is tied, to a certain degree, to wisdom which, in turn, is connected to one's intelligence. The lower auras may be developed by almost anyone who applies themselves but the key to development of the higher auras is soul growth. Only by dint of long years of prayer, meditation, and devotion to God can the higher auras be developed.

So it is that many spiritualistic mediums operate on their lower auras. They are limited, therefore, to explore those realms and the higher realms remain unsavoured. More importantly, the individuals that they tend to communicate with are those who, when on Earth, were considered ordinary. The information received tends to be trite and lacking wisdom. We do not criticise such mediums. They do a valuable job in bringing enlightenment concerning life after death to the world. They bring comfort to many bereaved but we point out that the student should not follow their example.

Strive to achieve soul growth and you will then speak with wisdom. Mention must also be made that it is not necessary to be holy in order to achieve the gifts of the spirit. The greatest black magicians who lived had the gifts highly developed and used them to the disadvantage of fellow man. In between the holy and the devilish are many states. Be careful if you contact a medium. Do not assume that they are necessary holy people. Many are but not all. Use your judgement and tread wearily.

It is, therefore, plain that those who work for the power of God and those who work for the power of evil, whilst they are at poles opposing, come very close at a central point, at a dividing line, between the power of good and those opposing forces. Thus, it is very easy to observe someone richly endowed with the power of God and also someone enmeshed within the power of evil and see that they are so. It becomes more difficult, however, the nearer and nearer they come to be what we might call ordinary people as they approach the dividing line. Thus, we must consider whether we act exclusively for the power of good or whether, sometimes, we might step over that dividing line and are used by the dark forces.

We must consider the types of action that would deem to fall into either camp. Let us, therefore, presume that we are working for God but that we are perhaps not the most shining example of a God-filled individual. Should such a person suffer from irritability, anger, jealousy, heartache, should anybody working for the power of God show any inkling of being less than perfection, the answer is, of course, yes. Even the greatest amongst us is not perfect. Would that we were. If we were, we would not be here. We would be at one with God. Thus, we would disappear into that great force called the Godhead and we would not be here to communicate knowledge to you.

By that very token, it presupposes that none of us are perfect however much we try. Some are tempted more than others. Some give way more than others. It is relatively easy to lock oneself away in a monastery on a top of a mountain and not be tempted by fellow man and to fool oneself that one is at the Godhead. That is not so. An advanced spirit would be able to go into hell if necessary and still not be tempted. But we presuppose that the majority of us have very much those human attributes with us that do indeed lead us into temptation.

The nature of that temptation was mentioned earlier and it is supposed, purely thinking in terms of hatred, jealousy, despair, and anguish, that being negative forces, should one feel them, one is acting in co-harmony with the dark forces. That is not necessarily so. As was mentioned, even the greatest of us suffer from those faults to a certain extent and yet we would assume that the greatest are squarely on the side of good. Therefore, should you feel those negative forces rising within you from time to time in response to temptation, we suggest that you attempt to put them to one side if you can rather than give way to them.

We want you to adopt a pose that enables you to recognise instantly when you are acting in an ungodly manner and begin to correct yourself immediately. Then, even though you have been tempted, you will still be acting in a godly manner because you will be trying to correct those faults. On the other hand, those whose souls still sleep would find that they would justify the reasons why they can give way to that indignation, those rages, those hatreds. They would justify them in terms of being correct in relation to some concept that they would argue and all around would agree that they are justified in so feeling. However, because that is so, there would be little or no attempt to correct or to reduce those passions and then, that person would be adjudged to be within the grip of the powers of darkness.

We hope, therefore, that you will get into that habit of examining your motives and your reasons for acting in any particular fashion and should you find yourself becoming angry over any situation, should you find yourself seeking justification for your anger, we ask you to remember always that you will be acting incorrectly. You will only be acting in the correct godly fashion when, and only when, you put aside any anger, any of the negative forces, and seek to maintain peace and tranquility within your heart. That might well be your watchword. The moment any feeling of peace and tranquility leaves your heart, be assured that you are acting in an incorrect manner.

The objective to which one strives is to maintain peace at all times within the heart. With peace, one can assume a state of prayer as one, through that prayer, recognises the power of God within oneself and within all things. That power and that prayer may become a part of your life until you lead a life, as has been mentioned in other publications, a life of constant prayer. It was the aim of Saint Paul and we suggest that you make it your aim also. But, you will not achieve such a state should you constantly give way to feelings of anger and any of the negative forces. Concern yourself only with peace and strive always for that. And so we recommend that you arm yourself through the trinity of prayer, meditation, and devotion to God. That is all that is needed to equip you with sufficient power to keep you firmly on the side of goodness. Then, no matter what shortcomings you have, you will still be able to keep your oneness with God.

We recommend also that you spend your time in a relaxed state, never becoming emotionally aroused, excited, or with inflamed passions if you possibly can avoid it. Arrange your life so that you have sufficient time to accomplish the things that you need to do and that you want to do. Ensure that you take sufficient rest and that you arise sufficiently early to enable a state of balance to be maintained in your life. If you find yourself hurrying, it is because you have been negligent in completing the tasks that you were assigned to do. To hurry is, therefore, to admit that you have not acted in a godly manner because nature never hurries. Nature knows what it has to do and allows itself sufficient time in which to do it. It then devotes its energy to completing that task and proceeds steadfastly towards completion. It is a human failing to attempt to undertake more tasks than can be successfully completed, to diversify on the grounds that one is achieving more when, in fact, one achieves less.

One should never be rigid. One should always be like the willow, swaying with the breeze, but, like the willow, we should concentrate our energies in one direction only at a time. If you think that you cannot do this because of the complexity of your life then it is suggested that you adjust your lifestyle until you have a minimum of diversions. When you go to your employment, act for your employer. When you return home, then act for yourself. Try to avoid mixing one with the other. Your weekends would best be spent in relaxation and rest to recuperate the energies that must be extended in the coming week. It is unwise to fill one's weekend with frantic activity as if to make up for lost time. You are merely losing more time by so doing. God will allow you sufficient time to allow you to complete any and all of the tasks that you wish to do. So do not hurry. Work diligently at all your tasks and you will find that your life will begin to run much more smoothly.

# CHAPTER 9 - THE BEGINNING OF SPIRITUALITY

It has always been supposed that man has had a relationship with Earth, that is to say that it has been supposed that the creature that we call man either evolved from the ape family or was created from the dust of the Earth according to whether you tend towards Darwin's theories or the Old Testament. In fact, both ideas are wrong as one would hope would have been obvious to the student who has followed the teachings in this book thus far.

Man's relationship with the planet Earth stretches back for many many years and his reasons for being here are greatly different from that proposed by Christians, Jews, and Muslims. It is frustrating when we know that the information now being expounded was made available to scribes and storytellers long years ago and yet that which comes down to us today in religious publications bears little or no connection with that original message, having been distorted by accident or by design.

We trust that, due to modern means of communication, this reprint of the story will never again be subject to amendment but will always remain in its virgin form. Then, further revelations may be made advancing the knowledge of mankind about himself and the planes upon which he operates instead of always having to return to basics and repair the damage in basic concepts perpetrated by mistake or fraud.

Darwin may be forgiven for his mistakes. He studied the animal and plant kingdoms with the only tools at his disposal – the five senses – and from his observations, he drew what conclusions he could. However, as has now been made clear, the five senses are merely a small part of the arsenal of measuring and quantifying abilities that God provides man with and that, by using these other senses, one can observe action taking place in areas unknown to Darwin. He merely observed the results of the manipulation of matter occurring in camera and so drew his conclusions.

That those theories are still expounded in schools, colleges, and universities today is, of course, an indictment of the insensitivity of those who teach. There should, from now on, be no excuse for teaching the youth of today, destined to become the teachers of tomorrow, theories that are not actually correct. It is beholden upon the teachers today to achieve the necessary soul growth themselves to understand that the information contained within the publications to be made available is both true and a complete package sufficient for the moral, spiritual, and intellectual growth of all students.

We are in fact proposing that teacher training colleges have a basis of spirituality, that as well as training would-be teachers in the techniques of passing on information alone, that they should also be given a thorough grounding in meditative and prayer techniques and that certificates of competency should not be distributed until each teacher has demonstrated that he has acquired a degree of wisdom, as defined within the term soul growth. We feel that such a day is, at the moment, far off, especially in countries where the education system is in the hands of and under the jurisdiction of individuals who have banded together to form an atmosphere designed to spread corruption amongst the youth of today.

We find it deeply saddening that the future of many millions of youngsters is controlled by such people and, although those corrupt individuals will pay a heavy price for their sins, nevertheless, there are generations of youngsters who reach manhood with no ability to communicate on any meaningful level whether by the spoken or by the written word, who have no ideas of the basis of brotherliness that all men naturally seek, and who feel no sense of respect for themselves or for their fellow man.

The results are all around for all to see – a breakdown in moral values, the collapse of law and order, physical abuse of self and others by drug taking and by violence, and a feeling of being lost. It must be very sad to be a young person being brought up in such a society where there is such an abundance of physical effects and such a paucity of spiritual guidance.

We appeal to all who can help reverse the situation to do so. Teach all who will listen of the correct way to live. Appeal to your friends to join with you in setting up nondenominational prayer and meditation groups. Spread what light you can by your example of godliness. It is unfair that those malign ones should wreck your lives, the lives of your children, and of your grandchildren, which is their hope. It is up to each individual to use the power of prayer in peace and in love to change the situation.

We look forward to the day when schools will be established teaching correct moral and spiritual attitudes; we look forward to the day when parents reassume their duties as mentors to their offspring, duty which has been taken over by the state in some countries; and we look forward to the time when people can be elected to parliament and the senate, to areas of political importance throughout the world, and for those so elected to act in an honourable spiritual manner, truly representing the best interest of the constituents in a manner quite unlike today.

Does all this seem "pie-in-the-sky"? It does at the moment, which gives you some idea of the strides made by the fallen ones. Do not suppose that you are powerless to remedy the situation. Providing, as was mentioned earlier, you are of strong character, you will flourish enormously under the mighty influx of prayer and if you can find two or three like souls, then act as Jesus begged 2000 years ago and bring the kingdom of God to the children of the Earth, children of all ages now.

We who dictate this information can only help to a limited extent. Our earthly lives have long since finished but we feel great concern for the mass incarnate and awaiting incarnation. It is an abomination to see such hopeful, bright-eyed souls born on Earth expecting, quite rightly, to advance towards God during their earthly stay and to see them much later as they give up the mortal-coil, lost and disillusioned and battered from the dreadful forces of maliciousness that play round them from the moment of birth to the moment of their release.

We feel great anger that such time, energy, and effort is wasted by the relatively few evil ones who control your lands and deny to all the knowledge and love, the freedom and happiness, that is your birthright. This situation will continue until you as an individual and you as a mass take control of your own lives and thereby put yourself in a position to bring freedom to those enslaved individuals. Do not think that you can achieve oneness with God, and live a life in happiness, in isolation from the suffering of your fellow man. Oneness with God implies oneness with all and your happiness will be tarnished by the sorrow of the suffering masses.

Seek God in the peace of your heart and in the quiet of your home. Seek out like souls and form small dedicated prayer groups. As and when you feel the strength, set up churches to teach the real truth of God. Set up Sunday schools. Establish with those qualified teachers who are at one with you, after-hours schools teaching basic education and communication. Ensure that each pupil knows, by your example and through your teaching, the truth of his relationship with God and so gradually alter the way that your community lives.

As these youngsters grow to maturity and have families of their own, encourage them to teach the correct domestic relationship between parent and offspring – parent, offspring, and God – and so establish a society that you will look back on with pride and pleasure when your turn comes to reach the spiritual realms. But, we want you always to be wary of the fallen ones. They often occupy positions of authority and power in local and central government. They may be found amongst the dignitaries of churches and they will occupy the authoritative positions in education groups.

Often, they do not realise that they are used by the forces of evil. They are usually not evil themselves. But, because their souls sleep, they are made use of by malign forces. They are successful and occupy top jobs because, in the degree they lack spirituality, they are of the Earth and, being at home in an earthly environment, they are at one with and able to manipulate earthly concepts to their own advantage. Thus, they graduate into top jobs and to positions where the evil that flows unconsciously from their lips and their pens spreads dismay, despondency, and mayhem throughout the world.

Be warned that, as you set up prayer groups and attempt to alter the path that they have mapped out for the masses to follow, they will react instinctively and with violence. You will be condemned by local and central government politicians and by leaders of churches. You will be accused by leaders of education authorities, of medical boards, and of those of any area that you encroach upon. Having been forewarned, make sure that you are forearmed. Play the game by their rules. Make sure that you are on safe ground legally before you act or they will condemn you and break up your organisation.

It is strange to think that, according to the Bible, the Egyptians tried to destroy the Hebrews, the Hebrews and the Romans tried to destroy the Christians, and now it is suggested that the Christians will try to destroy you. This gives you some idea of the power of evil and how beautiful concepts, such as the teachings of Christ, could be corrupted by evil and yet, in the year that this book is being written, we find that the home of Christianity, the Catholic Church is being rocked by allegations of corruption and by links with the mafia. Does this surprise you?

Well, if you have accepted the information concerning the power of evil given earlier, it shouldn't. It is almost inevitable that such events happened. It has happened because the organisation begun by Christ was changed from simple prayer groups and people serving mankind – Godly concepts – into a vast organisation which exists in its own right, completely divorced from and outside of the concepts of Christ. Perhaps, one day, the Catholic Church will open its doors to all comers, will sell their vast treasure and give to the poor, and will follow Christ once again.

But, we do not wait for them to change. We must set up organisations in the spirit of Christ and of God. Beware of any member of your organisation suggesting that you become a religion. Christ's relationship was with God direct. Your relationship is with God direct. You must not set up any organisation that purports to worship God through anything or anybody. The Christians have gone astray by placing Christ with God, put Christ as an intermediary between man and God. This is incorrect. Christ was and is as you. He is from God and is on a path to God. He is much further along the path but nevertheless he is still striving as you are. He did not see himself as an intermediary. Indeed, he exhorted all to pray direct to God. The prayer he wrote, the Lord's prayer, begins "Our Father who art in Heaven," not "His Father" but "Our Father". He made clear his oneness with you and his deference to God. He recognises that he is still separated from God and yet recognises God as his creator, as he recognises God as your creator.

Therefore, do not create religions. Should you do so, you will place a false barrier between yourself and God and, presently, you will create priests to mediate between that mediator and you. So, God will gradually become more and more remote. False teaching will creep in to protect the right of priests to act as mediators and to justify why man must not pray direct to God. Money will be collected to pay their salaries and to provide them with the splendid apparel and homes that their positions as mediators between man and God concepts require and, once again, we are back on the path to chaos that all established religions are on.

The key to salvation is sincerity of purpose, of simplicity, and of allowing all men the freedom to be at one with God. Do not establish religions. Do not wear strange garments. Do not perform any ritual. God is not impressed with silken robes hung with gold and jewels. He is impressed with honesty and sincerity of purpose. You might fool a gullible public by speaking in Latin or Hebrew, by swinging incense, by bowing and scraping, and by ringing bells, but God is not impressed. He would be impressed if you would assist your fellow man to meditate and to find God for himself. He would be impressed if those robes, jewels, gold, and silver were turned into money to feed a starving native of some country where man has not had the intelligence to provide irrigation, etcetera. So we beg you – always keep your faith simple.

Those experiences that you have and which mean so much to you might help others but they might be meaningless to others. The prayer that you find so effective in opening your heart to divine influence might be useless to another. All men are different and all men will develop their path to salvation independently. So freedom is the keyword. Allow each and every one the freedom to develop the path to God that they must do and allow them to develop at their own speed. Providing you provide the environment in home, in employment and in education, as was mentioned earlier, do not try to control the path and the thoughts of the individuals as they develop their relationship with God. You will, if you consider for a moment, merely be used by the forces of evil should you try to control the thought of others, for that is exactly what the politicians, church leaders, and all those used by the power of evil try to do.

We wish you luck in your newfound freedom. We wish you luck in the path that you will now follow and we ask you to remember that you are never alone. The power of God is always and ever present, as is advice from The White Brotherhood, which will continue to monitor progress and offer advice. Never think that you are isolated from the power of good. It is closer than your skin, nearer than thought, and always and ever present to assist you in your task. We seal you in the name of Almighty God and send you out into the byways and highways to complete the work started by Jesus and his disciples.

# CHAPTER 10 - THE LAW OF MUTUAL ATTRACTION

We now turn to consider an aspect of the growth of mankind that is limited to progression through the spheres of consciousness. We enter an area that is somewhat nebulous when considered in relation to the more mundane considerations that were examined earlier. We wish to think about the forces that attract man to Earth in the first instance and the forces that impel man on his journey through the planes that exist for exploration by man once again discarnate. Such consideration present concepts that will be quite difficult to explain and perhaps even more difficult to comprehend as they concern forces and events relatively unknown to normal thinking.

We must, therefore, begin by explaining that the forces that play round and through any material object, which is akin to gravity, is but a low form of a much larger concept that has far-reaching effects upon all life. That enigmatic force that is termed gravity has properties that have been explored and quantified for many years without anyone beginning to understand what it is. As is so often the case, scientists remark upon the effects of gravity and how that effect grows or declines in relation to the mass of a body and the distance between two bodies but have to content themselves to limit their investigations to that. The nature of gravity will not be easily understood as it relates to a fundamental law of like attracting like – the law of mutual attraction which is, as are all laws, from God.

If the laws of gravity are incomprehensible to man, you can imagine that to describe the law of mutual attraction in all its beauty and wonder will be an almost impossible task because language does not exist to describe some of the events occurring. However, let us assume that gravity is a force that exists within a body and radiates outwards from that body for a certain distance. It has been observed that the force is greater in a dense material and is termed mass. All that means, of course, is that some objects or materials have a greater amount of gravity within them than others. Thus, they are attracted to the surface of the Earth more strongly and appear heavier. Lead is heavier than a feather, the force of gravity being greater in lead than in a feather.

As to why any one object should appear to be heavier than another, scientists conclude that the atoms comprising that matter would be more tightly packed than in a lighter object. Therefore, the space between any two atoms would be less in a heavy object and greater in a light object. In fact, the space between the atoms is irrelevant as is the weight of any atom. The force that is termed gravity bears no relation to the number of atoms in an object nor how tightly they might be spaced. That theory is a futile attempt to account for the difference in mass between different materials and is incorrect. We will attempt to explain the nature of gravity which acts upon bodies and gives them mass.

The power of God is a force that is, in essence, a life force and indeed creates all that is. That life force is capable of many variations in its manifestation. It is seen in all live creatures and equally is in all inanimate objects. Thus, as has been stated earlier, all is related and all is one. That life force can be considered to be

100

at the heart of every atom and radiates outwards towards everything else. It is a law of God that in its drive to achieve oneness, it seeks to draw all matter to itself. However, it would be nonsensical if matter combined in a haphazard fashion. Therefore, the archangelic forces that control the life process endow matter with certain characteristics that permit order to obtain.

In the case of material objects, it was found relevant to endow atoms of earthly matter with an attractive force varying in strength from slight to great. This has enabled matter to combine into patterns that we see around us. The atomic particles that combine to make the structure of a bird are very light so that the bird might fly with a minimum of effort. The atomic particles that have combined to produce stones and Earth are heavier that they might be used by nature to support trees, etcetera. It is not the density of the atoms that matters, it is the degree of attractive force, the power contained within each atom, that varies and it is that which provides the concept of mass or weight.

Understanding of that relatively simple point will enable us to take the next step and begin to examine the larger, more far-reaching concept of how the law of mutual attraction acts within the life force, bringing together that which the life force requires in order to manifest itself on any plane and in any degree. Let us suppose that, once again, we examine our friend the daffodil. This plant is chosen purely at random. Any other plant, mineral, or animal would have provided enlightenment in the same degree. However, we have observed in an earlier chapter that the plant springs into growth, matures, flowers, declines, and apparently dies, although it is merely dormant. We have studied why this process is vital to the ongoingness of all life and it was appreciated that the battle between the forces of growth and the forces of decay perform a vital function.

Mention was made of the archangelic forces who manipulate for good the essential life force, the logos, of that plant in order to permit the species to evolve successfully in an ever-changing climate. From that basis, we will consider the nature of the force that draws matter, in all levels applicable to the plant, together to manufacture a daffodil as distinct from a rose or a thorn bush. We are accustomed to observe within the structure of any living thing a series of molecules termed DNA and RNA. We are informed that they are basically sugar in content and form the building blocks, the blueprint, for that plant.

We nod our heads sagely and turn away just as mystified to comprehend how, if the DNA of one plant appears basically identical to that of another, how then does the plant know that it is a daffodil or a rose or, indeed, a horse or a human? We will not find the answer by examining the molecules observable in a physical realm. That which is observed is merely the end product of a complex interplay of forces manipulated by those archangels who control the nature of all life. The real action is taking place in areas far removed from the aegis of the naked eye.

We, therefore, begin at the highest point in the construction of a daffodil. It is decided that there is a need to construct such a plant and so, from the bank of life force, a life essence is selected and endowed with the necessary qualities that will set it forever to being a daffodil. The nature of that force which gives undifferentiated life force a certain quality, as was mentioned before, cannot be successfully described. We ask you to accept that it exists. Once that life force has been endowed with the qualities needed to enable it to become a daffodil, then it begins a long journey downwards in terms of vibration towards the Earth. The essential life force does not alter in vibration but, as it descends, it draws around itself an aura of fine matter that is essential to permit it to identify with the plane that it is destined to land upon.

However, the question is, of course, what is the attractive force that causes matter to be drawn round the life force? This is the point that language begins to fail us. We have asked you to accept once the nature of a force that causes life force to become differentiated into any particular area and we do not wish to presume upon your credibility by asking you to accept more and more mysteries. We therefore will attempt by analogy to explain how a life force attracts particular forms of matter to itself, leaving all other alone.

Mention was made earlier of colours of the rainbow, of white light being split up into an infinite variety of tones and hues. We also spoke of the force of gravity being split into different levels of vibration resulting in one object being of greater mass than another. We carry on with the concept of layers, of levels, into which something can be split, ranging from whatever type of forces are necessary, from little to great. By the same token, the living force enwrapped round any living object is endowed with the ability to attract only the vibrations of a particular bandwidth.

Thus, we wish to present to you the concept that the life force destined to become a daffodil is charged with a force by the archangels that causes matter of a particular vibration to be attracted to it and that matter is necessary to the total creation of a daffodil. It is exclusively used for a daffodil and will remain in suspension despite all else that is made, awaiting the creation of daffodils. Therefore, we hope that you can appreciate that a simple, yet marvellous, life force within its coating called a soul is endowed with a force that not only tells it that it is destined to become a daffodil but sends out a signal at, initially, the highest level that alerts the mass of etheric matter floating aimlessly that it requires a certain amount at a particular vibration to be drawn to it. Thus, it assumes its first aura.

It must be appreciated that that description, though in essence true and graphic, is nevertheless a poor description of the reality. The beauty of creation will have to be experienced by the individual once he reaches a high enough level of advancement. Words cannot describe the creation of life any more than they can describe a sunset. We ask that you accept as a working hypothesis these words until you can prove for yourself the reality of creation.

The life force that we may now call an embryo daffodil slowly descends through the planes of ever denser matter until it is able to merge with the parent body of the plant in the Earth and a new bulb is born which will grow slowly until it is mature enough to flower and to contribute to the cycle of energy that flows in a rotating manner, enabling all life to progress.

Those who have followed the discussion so far will no doubt be curious to discover how the concept that applies to a daffodil relates to humans. Most of the events that occur in God's kingdom, called nature, are basically similar in that what applies to one piece of basic God-force in a particular circumstance applies to all. Therefore, it may be assumed that all life forms that were, and are, destined to be part of the Earth would follow the pattern of creation that was described earlier.

The life forms of the Earth would include all minerals, all atoms that create air and water, all vegetation, and all animal life. The sole remaining inhabitants of the Earth that do not fit into that pattern are humans. As has been mentioned earlier, humans are visitors to the planet Earth and their true home is in the spiritual planes. Therefore, the path that they follow to be born, to incarnate, is slightly different to that of the Earth forms.

In essence, the process is similar in that the differentiated life force with its soul coating would draw round it matter that would enable it to land on any of the planes of auric vibration and so finally to be born on Earth. But, there are a number of variations. First and most important, it should be noted that unlike the Earth forms, human embryo souls do not necessarily incarnate on Earth. There are many areas for humans to explore and to grow in stature and the Earth is only one of them. Many young souls feel the need to incarnate into gross matter but not all. It is quite possible to bypass the earthly incarnation stage. Do not believe the fall from grace story in the Bible. It is a misconception of why people incarnate on Earth.

Some, indeed vast numbers, of embryo spiritual beings have a propensity for good and so are not attracted to the Earth. Others, for whatever reason, sense within themselves that they are not naturally pure. This may seem strange to imagine that some souls are naturally pure and some are not but look around you. There are many men and women who lead decent lives and there are some who seek every kind of degradation. Therefore, accept the veracity of the information given.

Those individuals who sense that they are not naturally perfect would, automatically, through the law of mutual attraction, be drawn to a particular area for growth. In your case, and ours, it was the planet Earth. It could have been one of many other planets. Mars is an example. Scientists in their rocket ships have photographed Mars and have observed nothing. Unfortunately for them, they have been looking at the physical surface. Had they the ability to observe with auric vision, they would observe a great deal of activity and much of it unpleasant. However, we will assume that we feel attracted to Earth.

We descend through the planes of ever denser matter until we arrive at a final staging post, one of twelve, because remember that we travel along a ray that we call a sign of the zodiac. At that staging post, we rest. We have now round us not only our spirit of God within its soul, not only seven auras albeit rather limp being totally lacking in power, but also we now have an etheric double, a coating the exact replica of the human figure. During the resting period, we wait until we feel drawn by the same law of mutual attraction to a particular country, to a particular class and colour of people. We wait until a suitable couple conceive a child.

That child does not contain a soul at that point nor a spirit of God. It is an extension of and dependent upon its mother. It will contain within its genes certain characteristics of both parents which will, to a certain extent, form its body and facial characteristics, but its personality will be that of the incarnating individual. If that were not so and the baby merely responded to the genetic influence of the parents, all babies of any particular parents would be born identical and all would have the same personality. This is clearly not so except in the case of split eggs forming identical twins. Even then, they have their own individual personalities.

As the baby grows within the womb, the incarnating individual draws closer and closer until he is able to merge partly with the baby. However, he does not take complete control until the baby is born. At the moment of birth, the soul and etheric body enwrap themselves around that baby and it springs to life. Doctors think that by slapping the baby to force it to cry, it affects that process but, although it opens the babies lungs, it is the merging of spirit, soul, and etheric double that causes the baby to become alive. There are cases where the body of the baby is faulty in which case the spirit, etcetera, withdraws and the baby dies. But, in most cases, the baby is successfully brought into the world.

However, the auras do not all merge at once. To do so, the power required to pour energy in and out of the body would be too great and so the baby initially lies in its cradle with a body and etheric double, a soul, and a spirit. Gradually, over the years, the auras merge one by one, typically, every seven years. Therefore, the infant is relatively mature in years before it has all its auras and, therefore, it is not possible to be a complete human with all the attributes including wisdom, etcetera, until one is middle aged. You cannot indeed put an "old head on young shoulders". It is futile to attempt to do so.

In the old days, the youth did the hard work of the tribe and gathered the food whilst the elders sat in council, deliberating and formulating policy. This process followed natural events and was correct. Nowadays, it is customary to promote energetic youth into positions of power and authority. It is a mistake because they do not have the auras around them to allow them to make wise decision. The result is all around you and the chaos will remain until you relegate the youth to do jobs requiring strength and vitality and leave policymaking to the elders.

Those that allow themselves to come to terms with the need for change within their society will appreciate that it is necessary to follow the precepts of faith, love, and charity in order to realise oneness with God. There is no room for ego to manifest itself and there is no place for power struggle. Those concepts will drive men ultimately to despair because, should one carry those emotions along with one for sufficient time, they will create such disharmony within one that will cause great unhappiness. They must be got rid of and as soon as possible and then the auras may begin to quicken in vibration, to fill with energy and will alter the character of the individual.

We state the above to indicate that, once again, man differs from the plant and animal kingdom. The auras of plants and animals are not capable of expansion or contraction in terms of vibrancy because plants and animals are incapable of many of the higher and, indeed, lower emotions. The creatures of the Earth have a set of emotions that is applicable to them and are in fact alien to mankind, although man loves to give human attributes to animals. Fear is shared with the animal kingdom but that is learned from animals. Animals feel pain, heat, and cold. They feel affection on a par with many humans but that is but a poor reflection of the true emotion that can be experienced. All other feelings are applicable only to them. Plants are even more limited and soil, etcetera, yet more so.

It is, therefore, that the auras of those Earth beings do not expand greatly. Thus, they contribute little to the overall power available within the universe. However, that is the limit of their capabilities. Man should be capable of much higher, more powerful emotions and should be capable of filling the auras to a much greater extent. The overall effect upon the universe is therefore much greater. However, many, indeed most, do not fulfill their potential. They spend their lives in useless pursuits and contribute little to themselves or to the total stock of universal power.

It should not be so. Indeed, one of the reasons why man incarnates on Earth is to fulfill the quota of spiritual energy being emanated from the planet into the spiritual realms. By not doing so, man is therefore permitting an increasing deficit to be built up which contributes to the negative forces holding sway over the Earth. People often argue that conditions, generally, are worse today than they were years ago. It is true. It is because the spiritual deficit is ever increasing. Therefore, life will become more and more chaotic until those, who can, begin to pray, to meditate, and to serve God. Their auras will expand, the flow of spiritual energy will increase, and man will become at peace with himself and with all life around him. All life will respond to the positive forces being given out and the troubles will begin to lessen.

We will now look at an area that will give insight into the mechanisms at work behind the concept of movement towards perfection in relation to the law of mutual attraction and how it works, drawing us into areas of opportunity, and bringing guides and teachers into our compass. We know either from experience, or by having read, that as we turn towards God in a positive and creative manner, we need to pray, meditate, and to serve God manifest in all life. We know also that it is necessary, indeed inevitable, that our auras will expand, filled with spiritual power, and that, sooner or later, we will be actively guided by a teacher who may be alive and on Earth or may be alive and in the spiritual realms. That teacher will be usually the only contact that the student will have to those enlightened beings but the teacher himself will have an even more enlightened one who will be guiding him and so on in a chain. Thus it is that all pull together towards perfection and that also the message remains pure as each student in turn receives information and passes it unmodified to someone who depends upon him for guidance.

That chain of linked beings does not come about by accident. There is a force at work, mutual attraction, which ensures that like attracts like. By that law will one spiritual person be drawn to another. However, that chain will only continue to be forged as long as each member of the chain acts in a correct manner. Should one of the links become weak then the chain will be broken. Should that happen then, of course, it is necessary to find another individual with whom the chain can work for the desire is ultimately for all mankind to be linked into one unit, all working for God and, until and unless the members of the original group all work to their utmost, then nothing can be achieved. All are dependent upon each other. Any one person may break the chain and that impedes the progress of all.

Such a state is not permitted to continue for very long. Those beings whom we call enlightened are compassionate. They understand all the problems to which mankind is heir. They have, in their time, experienced and suffered those problems. Therefore, they will allow time for any individual to overcome problems. They concentrate all their vision upon the work of God and will allow nothing to impede that progress. The student should take notice then that he is welcome to join the chain of spiritual beings. He will be used to further God's power on Earth. As he grows in spirituality, he will be used more and more. He will, too, be used as a teacher to someone less enlightened than himself. By that method, and through the experience that he gains by serving God, he will become a greater, more powerful link in the chain but, should he falter, grow tired, or disinterested in the work, he will be dropped by the group once all attempts to help him have failed. Once abandoned, he will find it difficult to resume his place on the team as the trust placed in him by his peers would have been broken.

Therefore, let the student act in a calm and positive fashion, not taking on more work for the spirit than he can maintain. The work will continue for the rest of his existence and should be viewed in that light. The story of the tortoise and the hare is an appropriate illustration of the thoughts we have on that subject. It is very easy initially, when the gifts of the spirit first appear and one realises that he is able to assist people in a positive and much sought after manner, but it is, too, a temptation to undertake too great a commitment in terms of time and effort. Disappointment is bound to follow which will cause disillusionment to the individual concerned and will reduce confidence by the public in the credibility of the spiritual concepts being portrayed.

People look to their leaders for example. A leader must therefore not be weak. It is unacceptable to the public for a person to preach one thing and to do another. Consistency is vital to the ongoingness of The White Brotherhood and, should you wish to join, you will be required to act in a consistent manner yourself, not just for a few months or a few years but for the rest of your time on Earth and for all of your long residence in the spiritual realms. Further, you would be expected to improve and grow more powerful over the years as you take on an ever-widening band of pupils that will be drawn to you by the law of mutual attraction. You must not fail them.

Therefore, through prayer and meditation, you will come to realise the area of service that you will use in order to serve the God made manifest in man and, as you advance, so you will be expected to expand your horizons to include more people and a greater diversity of disciplines. Work slowly. Work thoroughly. Allow yourself time. You have all of eternity before you. Allow your spirituality to grow and, in the same degree, your ability to cope with spiritual work will grow. Follow the precepts, the advice given in the chapter concerning the manner in which to conduct oneself for health and for vitality and in peace become at one with us.

You are welcome and are sorely needed. Never feel isolated or alone. We are always close to you, unseen and perhaps unfelt but we are there, ever-guiding, ever-carrying you on wings of light as we, too, are carried by those eagles who are above us. In turn, you will learn to fly and will carry someone to salvation. Let nothing and no one dismay you or turn you from the path. The chain of spiritual beings that you join will become a mighty armour enshrouding all the world, defending the just from the invading forces of Satan.

Your link is as vital a part of that armour as the greatest forged by the highest and most powerful being in Heaven. All is one. You and he are one. Do not forget that. You and Jesus are one and the same. He is in you, a part of you, and you are part of him. Just as you would welcome Jesus into your life, ensure that you live and act in a manner that Jesus, too, would welcome as part of himself. You will be making great strides for yourself and for all mankind by so doing.

We now come to a discussion of the methodology of a return to simplicity and to discuss why life is so complicated for so many. If we consider primitive man who lived not only long ago but still lives in remote regions of the world, we find that society surprisingly complex. One would imagine that such people would fill their lives with the needs for shelter, food, and procreation as do animals and have little interest in anything else, but such is not the case.

We find, upon study, that there is a complex infrastructure of social inter-reaction of religion and superstition, a clear hierarchical order, and so on. We study such people and marvel at the complexity of their lives, of their ritual and dance patterns, and of their habits regarding gender, food, taboos, etcetera. Yet, we seldom bother to inquire why this complicated and apparently unnecessary, to our eyes, order came about. It seems very important to the people concerned and occupies a great deal of time and yet contributes little to survival of the individual. If we, civilised, were to be placed in their environment, we would be fully occupied merely in survival with no time and certainly no concern for the extraneous events which are so important to primitive man.

Therefore, we will investigate why these strange patterns of behaviour are there and how they originated. It will provide insight into our behaviour in so-called civilisation. The first aspect which needs to be understood is that mankind is not indigenous to Earth as are animals. As has been mentioned earlier, we use the planet Earth to gain experience and to assist the Earth in generating spiritual energy. Therefore, when we first arrived here many millions of years ago, it was not only food and shelter that occupied our minds but we had a memory of those areas in which we had dwelled before incarnating on Earth. In those areas, we do not have physical bodies and therefore we do not require food or shelter nor do we procreate.

Therefore, unless something else occupied our minds, we would live in a mental vacuum. Such, of course, is not the case. We would be fairly simple creatures at that point in our development and concepts of God, prayer, and service would be unknown but, nevertheless, there is the memory that we were created by God and that, through our descent through the spheres, we observed, albeit darkly, great beings, planes of beauty, and wondrous worlds. Therefore, it would be natural that simple and unable to comprehend as we might be, our thoughts should turn to those worlds and that we should try to reach out with our minds and imaginations into those realms. Such is not possible at the time to achieve with success but there is the need and desire to try.

By the law of mutual attraction, the emotions surrounding those areas are drawn to those who reach out and so the imagination is fed with the concepts mentioned above. Although the creatures, human but very basic and simple, try to fit these imagined concepts into a cohesive pattern, they are not able so to do and thus they are obliged to formulate ritual in order to express those imagined events. With time, the ritual becomes formalised into patterns of behaviour which fulfill a need and to which all are desired to conform. The ritual begins to assume an importance of its own and, finally, becomes settled into a pattern of behaviour, a form of civilisation which is justified on grounds that it is the obvious and normal fashion of behaviour.

When man incarnated to Earth, he had of course the problem of shelter, food, and procreation to deal with. Once that was overcome, he was able to look round to see if there was anything else to occupy his mind. The memories of his previous existence came flooding back and he was soon immersed with forming on Earth a civilisation similar to that which was complied with in his spiritual realm. It was modified, of course, to take account of his Earth environment but followed similar lines. Thus came into being the strange rituals that we see today.

If we look closely, we can observe that at the nub of all belief is a belief in a deity and that there are usually God's that are known, that control the environment, and who must be placated and encouraged through sacrifice and dance. One can observe immediately the parallel between the reality of a creating deity and the directors of life who control the Earth and all that is, though they act automatically and do not need bribing. Also, there is usually amongst primitive man a concept of evil, of a dark force, a devil, and there are taboo areas. Once again, we know that there are indeed dark forces and that hell is very real. Thus, we can observe a likeness to reality in primitive man's ritual and begin to comprehend that he performs it because the information is fed into his imagination by the law of mutual attraction from the experiences glimpsed long before.

It is the fact that it becomes stylised into formal routines that will lead us into the modern world, for there we observe that we still act in fashions that do not really stand up under open criticism, that we have strange unreal concepts of God, saints, and of angelic forces. We, of course, through our increased intelligence and ability to manipulate concepts, have stylised and formalised these events into acceptability but when you go into a Church, when you see the priests in their finery, the choir dressed in flowing gowns of white, etcetera, ask yourself, where did the ideas come from? Certainly not Jesus nor from any other prophet. They lived, and worked, in whatever clothes they had on. They had no temples dripping with gold and jewels. No.

The memory comes down from those ancestral events experienced as we came down by the law of mutual attraction. We saw beautiful things, we observed God-like creatures, and we feel the need to recreate them in our attempt to climb back up the spheres to the plains of beauty. However, that is not the way. You cannot dress up as a king and by so doing become a king, you cannot wear the apparel of an angel and become one by so doing, and you cannot assume the mantle of perfection and arrive at that state. It is imagination. It is childish.

When you were children, you played with toys. If you wish to become a man, put away your childish things and act like a man. You do not need the churches, the priests, and all the finery that exists. Sell it all and give to the poor. Follow Jesus and, through the trinity of prayer, meditation, and devotion to God, you will rise to be at one with the reality that is. Reality is far more rewarding than imagination. Wear the apparel of simplicity and truth and you will one day wear the garments of a God. Keep your faith simple. Avoid ritual, gestures, and mumbo jumbo. The primitive being in the jungle has no means of transcending it, but you have.

Those who dress up in cloth of gold, those who recite, ritualistically, prayers, and perform ceremonies as if to appease the Gods waste their time. Do not let them waste yours. Your work is too important. Your world is in reality. Live not in the world of illusion but climb the stairway to truth, freedom, and genuine experience. Your reward will be great and will have the ring of truth. You will not finish your life disillusioned and empty like so many who devote their lives, no matter how honestly, to chasing shadows. You cannot catch a shadow. You cannot experience imagined events. Therefore, do not try.

The truth is solid, real, and is within your grasp. Cease it with both hands and cling to it for the rest of your existence. You will be blessed and in turn, by showing others the way, you will again be blessed. That is the way the law of mutual attraction works, bringing illusions to those who seek illusion and bringing truth to those who seek truth. Choose for yourself.

# CHAPTER 11 - DICTATES OF THE HEART

If we try to imagine how emotions formulate deep within us, feelings and passions, we inevitably are drawn in our thinking and our expressions to an area which we call the heart. It is clear that we do not consider the physical organ, the heart, to be the object of our appraisal but that we are considering an abstract concept that uses, as its symbol, a shape with which we are all familiar. Does it ever occur to anyone to question why considerations of emotion like love, desire, and beauty should focus upon an organ of the body which is largely muscle and whose sole function is to act as a pump for the blood passing round the body? Do we ever consider why a brave man should be considered big-hearted? Autopsy would almost certainly indicate that the heart of the bravest hero and that of the most abject coward were of approximately the same size. Therefore, it is clear that we are speaking metaphorically and we refer to the heart when, in fact, we refer to something else with which we have no ability to quantify.

Let us examine in detail the events occurring in a human should he experience the emotion of "falling in love". The law of mutual attraction, like all of God's laws is ever and always at work – attracting like to like. As an individual reaches puberty, he finds that certain longings begin to manifest within him. He feels a sense of lacking, of incompleteness, which he satisfies initially by mixing with numerous friends of his own age at school and in leisure hours. Later, that circle of friends widens to include people of roughly the same age group but of the opposite sex. These people are drawn together by the law of mutual attraction, the sense of longing in each individual being the catalyst that binds them together.

Sooner or later, it is usual that one person feels drawn towards a particular member of the opposite sex. He or she reaches out emotionally and that pull is sensed by the desired one who is compelled to respond in a certain manner. Let us suppose that a group of young people of mixed sex meet regularly for social reasons and let us further suppose that a young man feels attracted towards a particular girl. He manifests his desire to become familiar with her on several levels of consciousness. In a physical sense, he may sit near to her, talk to her, and generally spend more time with her as an individual than with others in the group. His body will assume certain postures, now known as body language, which she would observe subconsciously whilst, in an auric sense, the power of mutual attraction is sending a call from one of his auras which will be received by the girl.

She, then, has to decide how to respond. Initially, she will be flattered by the attention and will respond automatically to his body language. The aura that has received the call for togetherness too responds automatically and positively for it is a natural law that like attracts like, and just as two magnets come together without questioning why, so a person responds to the call of another. So, at first, she is drawn towards the young man. If all goes well, they will come together and fall in love. However, the young lady may herself have cast an eye on another young man. Decorum prohibits her making overt gestures to him but her body language and her auric call would be sent to him and he too must respond.

The young lady is now in a quandary. She feels obliged, indeed is obliged, to respond to the first party and yet, she has a complex interplay at work with a third party with whom she may hope to achieve greater things. He may be more handsome than the first individual, be taller, stronger, richer, have better employment prospects, etcetera. What, ultimately, she will decide is anybody's guess. There is little logic in the way most people choose their partners and perhaps it is better that way. Once, however, she has made her choice, she will cease to respond to one of the boys. She will show this openly by word, by look, by body language, by action, and, most importantly from the point of view under discussion, she will not respond with her aura.

It was stated that the law of mutual attraction works automatically, bringing like to like but, like all of God's laws, it is capable of being manipulated by the mind operating at the correct level. Just as the first young man in our story reached out exclusively to the girl he fancied, so that girl, once she responds and devotes herself to him, would cease to respond to any other call sent out by any other young man. She does this automatically but it is under the control of her emotions.

The reason that this story was described was to indicate some of the ways in which humans operate in a conscious manner, and also subconsciously, and to lead us into an area that relates to love and attraction. That area is known as the "heart". More properly, we should state that there is a chakra, an entry point into the body that has its centre at the heart. It is often imagined that the chakras actually enter physical body. It is not quite correct. The chakras are an etheric opening or doorway for particular auras and, because they are of fine matter, could not enter the body. They actually have their entry points centred within the etheric double and it is that which relates closely to the human form. However, in essence, the effect is the same.

As, by the law of mutual attraction a young lady responds to a man, so their auras relevant to their chakras reach out and intertwine, so to speak. This mingling of two auras has an electrifying effect known in modern parlance as a "gestalt", which means "the sum of the whole is greater than the sum of the individual parts", which means that by joining the two auras together into one, because the law of mutual attraction has achieved its desired effect, spiritual energy is released which will cause electrifying and exhilarating emotions within each individual. We say it is love. To repeat and clarify, what is happening is that through the action of two people becoming etherically one, a payoff is made by nature.

The law of mutual attraction is constantly striving to achieve its aims. When it does so, energy is released, matter has been raised, and the effect is felt as love. It is a beautiful emotion. It makes the whole world seem right and good. It makes one feel like a giant. In later years, assuming the couple stay together, that feeling is accepted into normality and appears to lessen. It does not lessen. It is accepted and the mind turns to other things. One realises the difference should the partnership cease for whatever reason and he returns to normal. The sense of loss, of isolation, of grief and misery is keenly felt until that too is come to terms with and the individual accepts it. His life returns to a sense of normality again and he or she might possibly begin to seek new partners through the original act of joining a group from which he can begin to make selections and send out overtures. The law of mutual attraction never ceases to work.

The gestalt concept is of great importance to the world. It is the way energy is created. Without the law of mutual attraction and the explosion of energy released as a result of a joining, all life would die out. That action is occurring at all times in all things, whether they be mineral, plant, animal, or human. It is absolutely vital to life everywhere in the universe. The result of the gestalt is always beautiful. Life joining life always creates happiness and joy. In simple terms, just go into the garden and look. From the cold, dank earth, from the animal droppings, springs plants, flowers of the most incredible variety, pattern, form and size, colour, and beauty imaginable. Hold in one hand a piece of earth. Crumble it and see how unattractive it is. With the other hand, reach out and cup a flower. Study it closely. Really look with all your concentration at the flower. Have you ever seen anything so beautiful? Was anything man-made comparable to that flower?

As you release it and as you drop the earth, rise and stand still for a moment. What do you feel within you? You feel exhilaration. You feel your chest swell and maybe you will have tears in your eyes. You will feel love. What has happened is that you and that flower mingled your auras in common affection so the gestalt released energy which gave you delight and, also, similarly benefitted the flower. That is the reason gardeners spend so long tending their plants. They are constantly surrounded by heightened emotion. Most true gardeners are happy, contented people. It is suggested that you too might grow flowers.

However, it is not sufficient to hoe them occasionally, water them when you feel like it. You must, to obtain the effect described, care for your plants. Reach out and mingle your auras with them. The plant will respond and grow better and you will feel better. Similarly, pet owners who really care for their charges, obtain happiness. The love for each other reaches out and rewards everybody so involved tremendously. One wonders why any person would wish to hate another when, by loving each other and caring for each other, all are made happier.

Similarly, in spiritual healing, as the healer and patient join in the common desire to achieve wholeness within the patient, the patient must and does respond and the healer too benefits. Any would-be healer should, therefore, not merely go through the action of placing his hands upon the patient and stand bored for a few minutes and expect results. He must desire to reach out emotionally to the God made manifest in that patient in a similar way that two young lovers reach out to each other. The patient will sense the call and will respond. The energy released will bring a feeling akin to love experience and the patient will feel rejuvenated. Pure love is a noble emotion. It is not sullied by base thoughts.

In the young, procreation is vital to the retention of human life on Earth and so that love rapidly turns to thoughts of sexual union. This is natural and proper in the young when bodies are healthy and the individuals have the stamina to cope with the stress that young children place upon people. However, as we mature and as the necessary auras fully envelop us, it is normal to turn one's thoughts to higher matters, to feelings of peace and tranquility. Warlike tendencies are transmuted to feelings of brotherliness and reconciliation. But some there are who never mature. The thrill of first love remains uppermost in their minds and they spend their lives chasing from one partner to another in an attempt to recapture and relive the gestalt that occurs when two auras combine. To a small extent, they succeed. As they meet a new partner and join in sexual union, there is an exchange of emotion that causes feelings of euphoria but that is rapidly dissipated as each partner realises that sexual attraction is not love. Therefore, they are forced to find new partners in order to attempt to achieve satisfaction emotionally and, usually, are doomed to failure. This is not love and this is not the manner in which one should live.

It is not normal to live a solitary existence because humans are gregarious creatures and, equally, it is not correct to seek many partners. The norm is for a young couple to meet, to fall in love, to marry, have children, and grow old in togetherness and harmony. Of course, that is an ideal state and, like all ideologies, is not always achieved in practice. For one or more of many reasons, the partnership may not succeed in an ideal fashion in which case the individual who may be left would tend to follow the example given earlier and reach out for another partner. In such a case, it is inevitable that what is experienced is an adaptation or variation to the ideal which is also the norm.

Due to the fact that all is one, that which affects one affects all and, therefore, should the harmonious state that is considered to be the norm not be achieved in any single couple, then all of mankind is slightly affected. The happiness of everyone is slightly marred. One can, therefore, realise the tremendous importance that is placed upon the correct, perfect relationships between individuals as that relationship is influential in the balance of harmony and happiness to all individuals, and couples thus alter the balance of power between good and evil.

It is, therefore, suggested to all who seek partners that they do so with the utmost care. In Western civilisation, couples tend to meet in a haphazard fashion and either live together or marry to satisfy basic emotional needs. It is obvious that the chances of such an arrangement succeeding in an ideal fashion are slim. The divorce courts are full of the debris of unwise commitments by individuals who had no guidance on how to choose a partner.

In some Eastern countries, husbands and wives are chosen, marriages are arranged for financial and power reasons by parents who place no consideration upon the most fundamental factor involved in relationships: love. Divorce is not encouraged in such areas and so whole families are raised in relationships which are far from perfect. In some cases, love grows between the partners but in many, there is merely a sharing of space, time, and sexual relations with little or no love. This is obviously incorrect.

Unfortunately, youngsters are given little or no guidance in how to choose partners to share all of eternity with. This state of affairs is incredible. Vast sums of money are expended in advising children and adolescents on sexual matters, on family planning, on marriage guidance counsellors, and on divorce lawyers, but not one penny is set aside to enable information about the correct method for enabling the right choice of partner to be made. There are no classes in school, no high street bureau, and yet the process is so simple. Imagine how much suffering could be avoided if all couples, indeed, lived happily ever after and the divorce courts were empty, if the children's homes, now full of discarded offspring, were a thing of the past. Imagine how much all of humanity would benefit from having families living in peace and harmony.

The process will now be described and it is advised that all youngsters, both male and female, should adhere to this advice in peace and in patience, for, once the call is sent out by one person acting correctly, his ideal partner will respond. However, that prospective partner may be far distant, perhaps in a foreign land, and so there may be a delay of days, weeks, years even, until the call is answered and the ideal couple meet. Therefore, patience is required. You will know when the correct person destined to become your soulmate has entered your sphere of consciousness. The gestalt will occur that will instantly alert you to the truth.

Therefore, it is proposed that, should you be seeking a partner, you sit quietly, close your eyes, and in simple everyday terms, ask God to open your heart and send the call that will bring your ideal partner to you. That is all you need to do. Once you have sent the call, thank God for the fact that the call is already winging its way to the destined one. There is no need to repeat the message daily. God does not need reminding. Therefore, send the message once and thereafter spend your days in a state of readiness, awaiting the answer to your call. It will be answered sooner or later.

116

There is much incorrect thinking concerning the term "soulmate". It has been suggested that the spirit of God that is made into humans has a duality, a positive and negative, which is made into two people, one male and the other female, who spend their lives in a search for each other, stumbling through relationship after relationship until they meet by chance. This is nonsense. The power of God, which creates all life, creates everything as individual. You are not part of a duality. There is no mysterious other half somewhere blindly seeking you as you blindly seek him or her, but there is someone, somewhere, who is by chance an exact foil for your personality. Indeed, there may be more than one.

If you consider for a moment, you have a particular personality that is the result of the ray that you travel plus the experiences that you have gained along the route and, in addition, genetic influences gained from your parents. That has given you a particular personality which, whilst unique, is and must be similar to that of many other people throughout the world. There are a finite number of permutations of personality but an infinite number of people. You can rest assured that there is someone somewhere in the world whose personality is similar to yours.

Equally, there are people whose personalities are diametrically opposed to yours. It is often supposed that people with opposite personalities should marry, each personality aspect being balanced by an equal but opposite personality trait in the partner. That too is nonsense. If you have ever encountered anyone who thinks completely differently to you, whose views on everyday affairs, on diet, on politics, on religion, on behaviour, are the opposite to yours, you quickly discover that communication is impossible as you have no common ground to share experience on. By that token, you would realise that your ideal partner would be a replica of yourself, not physically, but from a personality aspect.

Our old friend, the law of mutual attraction, of like attracting like, will ensure, should you ask, that any and all of the opposite sex with personalities similar to your own will be drawn to you. You do not need to wait until half a dozen prospective soulmates are in attendance before making your choice. The first one will be quite sufficiently close to you to provide you both with a harmonious existence for all eternity. For, make no mistake, a relationship under consideration is not expected to endure simply for your human incarnation but is required, and should, create an atmosphere of love and harmony for all of your long existence on the road to God. The simple act of asking God to help you find a soulmate should, and will, create a bond between yourself and your partner that will endure forever, bringing joy to you both and joy also to those who come into contact with you.

Remember that all is one. If you are happy, everybody benefits. If you are sad, the whole world saddens too. Thus, the matter of choosing a mate is simple. However, there are a number of areas and events that complicate matters. The first to be considered is this. Until now, few had the knowledge that you now have on how to arrive at a successful marriage. Therefore, you may already be married to someone who is not correct for you and does not bring you the contentment that is correct.

Further, you may have children. It is not the wish of The White Brotherhood to cause dissension between any couple or any family. Life will bring experience to all in any circumstance. Life uses every situation to provide a platform for experience for someone. Therefore, we wish you to understand and appreciate that even though you consider yourself married to the wrong person, that relationship is not a waste of time – far from it. It is providing valuable experience for you both: experience of the results of making wrong decisions; experience of learning patience in trying conditions; experience of seeing the other person's point of view even though it be the opposite of yours. Further, there will certainly be souls awaiting incarnation, in the very family atmosphere that you have, who need the experience of an abrasive domestic situation.

It is suggested that, if you consider that you have married incorrectly, you will talk the matter over with your partner in the light of the information given above. Not every person on Earth has the spiritual development to appreciate the wisdom given, and if that applies to your partner, then you must respect that point of view. However, should you both be able to comprehend how the laws of God operate, then discuss your relationship and pray for guidance. It may be that you will decide to divorce. That is up to you both. If it is so, ensure that it is a decision of you both based upon Godly concepts and not merely because one of you has found someone else more sexually exciting.

A marriage between two people based on love should, and will, endure forever. If there is no love, then there was never any marriage. You may choose not to divorce. That is the path recommended by the Brotherhood. Your relationship will endure for your physical lives. Should you have married at the age of 20 and should you both expire at the age of 80, your relationship will have lasted 60 years. That may seem a long time but if you can appreciate the meaning of the term that you will live for all of eternity, then 60 years is not too long. Once you are freed from your earthly environment, you can search for your soul mate and spend the rest of eternity with that person.

The reason that we recommend that you remain together is to allow you to benefit from the experience, as was mentioned earlier. Also, should you have children, you have a duty to nurture them towards God and they will not be in the best environment in a broken home or in an institution. Provide the best environment that you can for your children. We repeat and stress that. If you consider your relationship with the partner to be a mistake, then discuss it with that partner. Pray together for guidance. Should you decide to divorce then so be it. Should you decide to remain together for your earthly existence then try to find common ground where you can share happiness. Understanding of the process occurring within you will allow you to rise above these limitations and permit you to combine in some sort of partnership if you try. You have a duty to yourself and to God, and indeed all life, to be happy if you can. Try and be happy together in a give and take relationship. Who knows? Love may yet blossom if you give it the chance.

Some there are who are destined to live alone. They have chosen that path for their Earthly incarnation and, no matter how hard they try, they would not be able to have a successful relationship. To do so would be to fly in the face of their own karma. Once again, should you be single and find relationships difficult to maintain, pray to God for guidance. If you are meant to marry then, eventually, a partner will appear. If you are not, you will remain single. It is not normal for humans to live solitary lives but there are, from time to time, individuals born who have chosen that path in order to complete a set of experiences or to allow them to be free to complete some particular work that they have set themselves. Pray to God and you will be informed of the future that you should follow. Follow it in peace and in God and in the certainty that once your Earthly incarnation is finished, then you will re-join your family and friends in the spiritual realms.

Another group of people who do not normally fit together with ease are those who have travelled through time in a working partnership serving God and who have decided to incarnate together to further God's work on Earth. These people may not be soulmates in the accepted sense, indeed may have widely differing personalities, and yet may succeed in a harmonious, if stormy, relationship as they seek to serve God made manifest in man. Such people, as may all, may be born many miles apart and may spend a number of years in searching for each other, but eventually they will meet and their work will begin. Theirs may not be the most harmonious of relationships but because they work for the good of others, they will subjugate their personalities to the needs of others and so the relationship will work. These people may incarnate again and again, either in pairs or as individuals in their desire to serve God in man and it is implicit in this that they are spiritually more mature than most people on Earth at any one time. Their path is different from most people's and they live by different rules. They provide service to God and all are blessed by the work that they do and by the benefits that receive as reward.

We must now consider homosexual people. Traditionally, public opinion sways from abhorrence to acceptance of these individuals who feel most happy with an emotional and sexual relationship with members of their own sex. We will consider the rights and wrongs of homosexuality and what the attitude of society should be to such people.

Let us state that embryo spirits of God are non-sexual as are very mature beings. Before we develop fully into active humans, long before we incarnate on Earth, there is no question of sexual identity. We are merely human and content so to be. Similarly, once we mature to the point that we could be called wise, we no longer take any interest in the sex that we adopted in order to incarnate on Earth. The point where we begin to take an interest in what sex we are to adopt is when we arrive at one of the twelve etheric staging posts before incarnating on Earth. Because we need to experience certain events in order to help us mature, we realise that we will need to adopt a certain persona and sexual gender.

During our stay in the spiritual realm, that we call the etheric, we, as was mentioned in another chapter, seek a suitable host family. When that family decide to have a child, we pay close attention and should that baby have the correct attributes, we remain close to it and influence its growth to assist it to become either male or female. It is suggested that the gender of an infant can be influenced by time of day, by drugs, or by a number of other events and influences. It is not true. The spirit awaiting incarnation influences the embryo in the womb to become the sexual orientation that the spirit requires. Under normal considerations, the baby is born either definitely male or female.

However, as we know, some are born in a body of one gender whilst the incarnating soul considers itself to be of another gender. Therefore, we assume that something has gone wrong in the plan. The events that decide the gender of a baby are simple in that, in conjunction with the ubiquitous directors of life, rays are directed to the embryo baby that will cause it to tend towards male or female. However, nothing in life is perfect and there is a tendency for the genetic makeup of the parents to give the baby a sexual orientation.

There are other influences such as the phase of the moon which subtly influence the baby also. The result, sometimes, is that, for instance, a male baby might be required whilst in fact a female baby is born. Once it is realised in the etheric realm that something has gone wrong, one of three choices is made. Either a new soul of the same sexual drive as the baby is found or the baby is left without an incarnating soul in which case the baby will die or the original person incarnates. If the first event happens, then there is no problem. If the second happens, the baby is stillborn, which causes unhappiness to all for a while, whilst, in the third case, a homosexual is created.

We can see from the above explanation that homosexuality is not some perverse and wicked punishment wreaked upon an individual as some would suggest. It is merely a person making use of a body to avoid waste but that person, and the body that he incarnates in, are sexually opposite. This state of affairs can surely be understood and appreciated. If it were, then the individuals concerned would fit into society and gain from the experience. However, no one has bothered to find out the events occurring which cause homosexuality and so they are either treated as objects of disdain and scorn and abuse, persecuted and killed, or, more rarely, they are treated with reverence, are made into demigods.

They are neither. They are ordinary people in the wrong body from which they can learn a lot and from whom we too can learn acceptance. However, it must be noted that this state is not natural and there come into play a number of emotions that are peculiar to that state and also a number of diseases that would not normally occur. We state with force, however, that should you be a homosexual, you accept the situation and proceed on your path to God, all else notwithstanding, and if you know a homosexual, that you accept him as you would a heterosexual. All are from God and all are part of you. Accept all life and everybody will benefit.

The situation is quite different, however, in the case of a person who deliberately sets out to follow a path to God at an early age. We think, of course, of Buddhist priests, of Catholic priests, and of devotees to certain religions that proscribe sexual activity in their leaders. The act of restraint in a sexual sense causes a number of emotions to build within the framework of any who follow that path and those pressures are not always beneficial. Sexual frustration causes an imbalance, psychologically speaking, which is unhealthy to the individual and unwise in a spiritual advisor of men.

As has been stated several times, it is not normally considered "normal", nor beneficial, for humans to live solitary lives. That implies also that emotional relationships between members of the opposite sex should normally grow and sexual union is a natural result of such attachment. It assists the development of the power of God by releasing energy and, in turn, benefits the individuals concerned by raising their spiritual energy. The resultant effect is that the couple should be happy and all around them should have their spirits raised by contact with the happy ones. Should individuals choose to join a religious organisation which prohibits marriage, but the individuals require and need companionship and sexual relations, then conflict, inner conflict, occurs.

The manifestation of this conflict would be seen as irritability, poverty of spirit, and an unwillingness to spend time serving their flock. Should this occur in a priest or a nun, then it is obvious that the person would not be considered to be very suitable to advise others within the community who might require a great deal of patience, time, and love in order to deal with the problems that their path through life has presented. In defence, should one point out to any priest, monk, or nun of any celibate order that it is perhaps an unwise course to follow, they will argue that the founder of their religion – Jesus, Buddha, or whoever it might be – was celibate. It would, no doubt, come as great shock to many such if they could cast their minds back through history and view the Earthly incarnations of the founders of their religions as well-balanced individuals who experienced all that God provided and still were able to perform great deeds that history noted.

Time has formalised and stylised the lives of many great spiritual people out of all recognition of the truth that they themselves experienced, and one of the myths that time has created is that celibacy leads to godliness, or rather that the path to God is blocked by thoughts of sexual attraction between man and woman. Use your common sense to discover the truth. Do you think that a person full of sexual frustration is the best servant of God?   Would someone who had never experienced love, marriage, family life, and all the rich pageant  that normal people experience really be in a position to advise, to say, "I know what you are suffering because I too have suffered," as opposed to saying "I know how you feel because I read about it in a book." We therefore suggest to you that you follow the dictates of your body and your emotions in relation to God. There is absolutely no point to be gained from sexual abstinence unless you feel that you do not require sexual contact yourself. The so-called benefits apparently gained by such an act are, by far, outweighed by the detriment caused by emotional upset.

God's plan is for all people to live together in love, peace, and harmony. The family atmosphere developed by two people in love with each other and in love with God is the ideal setting in which to raise children. Those children, hopefully, will, when adult, commit themselves to a lifetime of devotion to God and will in turn marry and raise children in a like atmosphere. Thus will the word of God spread in truth. There is never any need for ascetic disciplines on the road to God. So follow God and, if you feel the desire, enjoy it.   A normal sexual life that encompass godliness and normality. We do not recommend excess in any area of life. That which deep inside you know to be right is the norm for you to follow. Always keep to the old adage, moderation in all things, and you will be working within the framework that children of God should adhere to.

The spiritual aspect of sexual harmony will benefit yourself and your partner and by implication all life will benefit. Ensure that you follow, through prayer, the precepts that the word "love" implies. Then you'll always be at one with yourself, with God, and with all life. That oneness is at the heart of the search for God. Seek God in everything and all will be one.

Should those of you who are yet bachelors require sex to satisfy natural sexual urges, who is to condemn you? The demands made by a healthy body require satisfying. For too long has sexual relationship within marriage been blessed and encouraged by orthodoxy and yet, the needs of single people, both male and female, ignored. And yet the young, normally, have strong sexual urges. The result of suppression of sexual urges is a distortion of the emotional content of that person resulting in action being taken in a different avenue. We note that many young men release sexual frustration in bouts of drinking and fighting. Girls, similarly affected, often turn to work of some kind such as business commitment or politics, when, if they had a natural sex life, they would be happy to spend their time in more suitable pursuits.

Therefore, we who advise you seek to present to your comprehension a declaration that we consider that, even outside of the concept of love, sexual gratification is realised and agreed as necessary. But at the same time, we do not wish to be misunderstood as saying that you have carte blanche to perform casual sex with any number of partners that base desire might seek. There is moderation in all things and the reason that moderation is required is that the aura of a person reflects his desires and his actions. These, in turn, raise or lower spiritual energy, and to accord with those emotions, it is necessary always to be in a positive frame of mind which cannot happen should abuse of the body and mind take place. Common sense is required and that will enable you to act correctly. Do not fall prey to lascivious thoughts. Enjoy sexual relations in happiness, in simplicity, in harmony, and in love, ensuring that you keep your focus upon your goal, which is oneness with God. By that aim, you will enjoy life as it was meant to be enjoyed and will still keep your mind pure.

The concept of purity of mind extends beyond the limitations imposed by accepted theories and dogmas in relation to control of thoughts. The term "purity of mind" can and does require action to be taken to purge from one's personality all thoughts and actions that would be considered to be in contradiction to oneness with God, God in Heaven and God incarnate in man. The idea behind the term "purity of mind" is to create, within the framework of which a human consists, a developed force that is squarely at one with God, leaving aside all possibility of separateness created by wrong thought or deed. That concept is not easy to put into practice, particularly whilst one is incarnate on Earth, for one is put into situations many times each hour that tempt one to think thoughts less than pure.

If there was the opportunity to retire into an area of peace for a sufficiently long period of time, it would be possible to bring the level of consciousness up to that required, where peace of mind inherent in purity of mind would obtain and could be maintained in the face of onslaught by evil emissaries attempting to distract love from the area of tranquility and godliness. Eventually, of course, one's defences would be battered down and then thoughts of corruption would enter, causing one to need to retire into an area of harmony with God to recharge the spirit. Fortunately for us, there is such an area, a haven, to which one can, and should, retire daily in order to release the spiritual power that will ensure total control of emotion and thought.

That area is the mind and the process for entering is "meditation". The process was described elsewhere and reference should be made to that section if there is doubt of the technique or procedures to use. Daily meditation is vitally necessary for all who wish to have purity of mind. What happens, within the mind during meditation, is that the path between man and God is laid bare, the gates opened and barriers lowered. Personality and ego, which normally shroud the mind like a prison wall, keeping God out and the mind prisoner, will be forced to step aside as the light from God bathes the mind in purity and love. The mind will absorb some of that power and will grow in stature and in purity. The power of the ego will decline in the degree that the mind absorbs spiritual energy from God and, eventually, should the disciple continue to meditate each day for long enough, ego will disappear and, although personality remains, it is now a God-filled personality shining with the power that bathed the mind. Thus will there be purity of mind, of heart, of spirit, and the individual so endowed will become at one with God as he becomes a reflection of God's power.

That power may be sent to others in meditation as a healing force and may be used to assist others in purifying themselves. Whether that power is accepted into the minds of others is of course dependent upon their abilities to push ego and personality to one side and allow their minds to be bathed with God's power. Please note that we stated that God's power may be reflected from a pure soul and directed towards others. The power of God does not come to anybody directly from God. It requires objects and/or people in order to manifest itself. Without living things, whether they be humans, animals, plants, rocks, or atomic particles, the power of God can only exist as a potential, a principle. It cannot exist in reality. It is always passed through, or more correctly, reflected by, material and living things. In the highest spiritual realms, the power of God is directed by those archangels we term the "directors of life" towards other creatures.

As has been mentioned before, the point at which the power is created and by what means, is not known. However, it does exist. It exists at the highest point of creation. The directors of life take that power, they are the first to manipulate it and they direct it towards its chosen destination. That destination might be Earth or it might be any one of a vast number of areas. Because the directors of life are without sin, they act as perfect reflectors and the light shines undiminished. It will be picked up by those who seek the light at the next highest level and would be reflected from them to those lower down the scales of life. It will ultimately shine towards you.

If you are fuelled with materialistic thoughts, your personality under the control of ego, will prevent you from absorbing that power and it will be wasted. However, should you follow the advice given earlier and meditate regularly and correctly, the ego will diminish and the mind will be bathed in the radiance emanating from God. It will then seek to be reflected from you to someone else in the hope of bringing enlightenment to all the world. This presupposes that you realise that you must reflect the light to others. If you do not know this, then the light, having helped you, will thereafter be wasted. So, it is necessary to direct the light to others.

In order to do this, it is not necessary to have a directory of every living soul in order to recite their names. It is sufficient during meditation to "will" the light to others, blessing all the world in God's name. That point of light that you were instructed to visualise will flood your mind. You will see it with your imaginative facilities because your physical eyes will, of course, be closed during meditation. However, you are not imagining that light. You are using the same areas of consciousness that imagination uses but the light will be real. During each meditative session, visualise the point of light and eventually, you will be flooded with pure white light. Do not strain to achieve this stage. Do not try to visualise it. It will come to you in its own time as you develop the meditative technique.

As you continue to meditate more and more, so you will be flooded with this brilliant white light more frequently and, eventually, you will be able to visualise it instantly as you begin your meditation and hold it in your consciousness at will until you finish your session. Later, you will learn to visualise the light during your normal routines and you may be bathed in it for all of each day. That state is recommended as bringing great joy and power to the student.

Should you meditate in groups or should you compare notes on meditation with your friends, take heed not to boast that you be the first to see the light. It is not a competition. Through thoughts and deeds, help each other. If you boast, you will encourage others to state that they too have achieved illumination when, in fact, they might not have. To lie is a sin. Do not put yourself in the position of sinning or encouraging others to do so. All will suffer.

As was mentioned earlier, that light, once seen, should be directed at random to all the world. Even those who harm you should be bathed in the light. It will reflect from you in the degree that you are pure. If your mind is soiled, you will not reflect much light. It, therefore, behoves all to become as pure as possible. Meditation and prayer will purify you. Perform it each day and ensure that you do not sin if you can avoid doing do.  Examine your faults and dismiss them. Do not dwell on them. To dwell on faults would be to increase their power over you. Take charge and dismiss them from your life. Actually examine your thoughts and words, your deeds and motives, all day long. Any act, word, deed, or thought that is not pure should be rescinded.

Gradually, you will purge yourself of fault. Your mind will become pure and you will reflect God's power undiminished by your flaws. That light will be picked up by someone else, somewhere in God's kingdom, and will be reflected to go on and on purifying all. It is important that you are pure of mind because, if you are not, you cannot absorb God's power and you cannot do God's work nor can you be happy and contented. The kingdom of God will be closed to you by your own thoughts. It is important, too, to be pure of mind in order to reflect God's power undiminished to others. You received it in full strength. You are required to send it on its way at full strength.

You can see from the above that the power of God, His light, does not come to you directly from God but comes via many life forms. That is because all is one.

You and your mind is part of everything and everybody's mind. It is called "universal mind". Through purity of mind brought about by diminished ego, you attune yourself to universal mind. Through that, may the storehouse of knowledge, the secrets of the universe, be revealed to you as you tune into that grand concept. Through the action of purity of the mind, the auras swell with power, God's power, which is universal power. The aura that is attached to your heart chakra swells and, because it has done so, the emotions involved with it increase. Those emotions may be termed universal love, because, although one may define them as happiness, tolerance, understanding, compassion, etcetera, they are subsets, so to speak, of an all-embracing force – love.

Man experiences love when he becomes involved with the girl of his choice who in turn responds to him. That love, whilst important, is poor indeed compared with the universal love to which we allude. It cannot be imagined nor can it be pretended. It develops within one as purity is attained. Purity does not mean incidentally the strange twisted puritanical concepts where physical love is regarded as dirty, where natural bodily functions are not considered, where nakedness is abhorred. We talk of a concept different indeed from that. We talk of a relaxed and peaceful state in which all thoughts of violence, greed, lust, are not considered, indeed do not any longer exist, but where acceptance of all is appreciated. It is a calm and submissive state where, even during sexual union with one's beloved partner, purity still exists.

Should that state be attained, then everything becomes pure. Everything is from God and cannot be unclean. It is our appreciation that is unclean. Purify the mind and all will be pure. Love all mankind and you will be loved by everything and by everyone. The light that you will come to visualise in meditation and which you will learn to carry with you all your days will ensure that you see everything and everyone bathed in its glow and all life will sense it and respect you.

The quality of your life will transform you as you align yourself with the power of God. The riches of Heaven will become yours. With God's riches, you will have no need to seek greedily the riches of the Earth. God will provide you with all that you need. Therefore, we urge you – no, we require you – should you wish to be accepted as one of the White Brotherhood to meditate daily, in peace and in love. By stating that you must meditate daily, we also ask you to use your common sense. If you are ill, if you are too busy, or too tired, then of course you cannot meditate, but try to arrange your life so that you have time to meditate once a day. You may do so more than once a day if you wish.

Eventually, you will reach a stage of permanent meditation but, initially, once a day for a few minutes or half an hour is sufficient. There will gradually come into your life changes that will alter you as described above, and we promise you, you will never regret them. You will only ever regret receiving this information and not acting upon it. Seek to align yourself with God and all else will be added to you. So let it be.

# CHAPTER 12 - PERSONALITY, ITS ASPECTS & ATRIBUTES

There are many forms of life created by God throughout the universe and surprisingly, they all have a number of common attributes. Such is the nature of life that it is not only related through the common source of creation but it is related too by those attributes that result in common purpose. There is only one source of creation, God, and there is only one destination for that creation. All life is on a cyclical voyage through creation which will result in those life forms, finally merging with the Creator. Everything returns ultimately to God.

Also, we find that all life is conjoined by a common reaction to a number of natural laws of God. We have previously examined the law of mutual attraction and discovered that that law was and is the cause of everything visible and that exists in the realms outside of human interrogation. Therefore, we may state that if everything that is reacts to a common law then those life forms must share a common ability to so react. Further, we find that the more that matter and created forms are examined, the greater the similarities and common attributes there are. Finally, although two life forms may appear widely different to our casual gaze, we find to our surprise that, in reality, there is less and less difference between them as we investigate and uncover the similarities.

We will ultimately find, should we have the means to comprehend, that there is actually no difference between any two objects. The difference in shape, form, constitution, etcetera, that we were able to quantify break down upon closer examination until the differences disappear and we realise that even should we examine two objects as widely differing, exterior and appearance as, say, a stone and an angel, that those differences are a result of the manner in which we perceive them and not the differences in the life forms themselves.

Is this a logical conclusion to which we feel drawn? Mankind has spent long ages quantifying the differences between similar objects and there have been forums of debate that have argued, for instance, whether two human beings, one white and one black, each had a soul. This was one of the excuses for slavery and yet it must be obvious now that human beings regardless of colour are virtually identical in all respects. Scientists, biologists, geologists have built careers and have achieved high fame in quantifying the minute differences between stones and rocks, plants of all kinds, and the delineation of material objects of all kinds. Museums are stuffed full of exhibits, all carefully marked for examination, where students may go to examine the exhibits so that they too may recognise the differences often so minute as to require sophisticated tests to delineate the differences.

Have you yet seen an exposition purporting to demonstrate the common connections between all things? And yet, we know that everything was created by God. Our information is that the power of God is one and the same as it is used to create different objects and so, for a start, the most fundamental substance at the heart of any material thing must be the same. As was mentioned earlier, all things follow a common path from creation to termination and do so by following common laws. The laws have a common source – God – and we find, when we are able to comprehend, that this logic, if followed to a conclusion, leads us to the truth that all is one. There is only one life force. There is only one path for life to follow. Even though there are a number of laws, their Creator is one and the same and all life operates according to those laws.

We realise that the more we learn about life, its creation, and its destiny, the more we come to the only possible conclusion that all is one. You and I are one. We are part and total of all that was, is, and ever will be. However, it is clear to you that you are different from any other person, animal, plant, or mineral. However much you try to accept the concept that you, the greatest archangel in the universe, and the humblest microbe are one, you still know deep within you that you are separate. You can pick up an object, say, a book, read it, put it down, and walk away and know that you and the book are two separate entities. How can this dilemma be solved?

We cannot make you feel at one with all that is because the stage of separateness that you feel is important to the stage of advancement that you feel. For instance, should a little fish in the ocean try to approach a shark in an attempt to relate in a brotherly fashion to that shark, the result would be that the shark would have an easy meal. Similarly, you live on the surface of a planet where creatures, including man, that have knowledge of their common source of origin are few indeed and should you lower your defences, you will be swallowed up by the dark forces that lurk close to you, watching and waiting for weakness in order to strike. Nature has put a shield around you to protect you from the ravages of life, to enable you to exist as a viable human, and to relate to all life for the number of years of your earthly incarnation. We do not ask you to lower that shield completely until you are able to build another even more powerful in its place.

Your original shield to which we refer is called the ego. Some psychologists, in an attempt to quantify emotions that play within a human, put a different meaning to the word ego to that which we refer. By the word ego, we mean aspects of personality that separate you from anybody and everything else. We refer to a sense of personal identity, of pride in self, of drive to achieve. We refer to the conditions in man that cause bloodshed, war, hatred, and disharmony. Those attributes are initially defensive and were given to you in order to permit you to survive. Out of control, of course, they become faults of aggression. However, you may rest assured that you have within your personality sufficient of the attributes of ego to separate you from all that is. Those attributes that constitute ego are necessary, and indeed vital, to you as you pass through an incarnation on Earth but of course they have no practical use once that incarnation has terminated.

Survival of the physical form is necessary in order that an individual might inter-relate with the environment and that he might experience inter-relationship with fellow humans who, for the first and last time, can act in a fashion that is unique to the planet Earth. Life, or rather body, may be taken during one's stay on the planet of materialism. That unique concept brings with it the unique requirement of the need to protect the body from assault by nature and by man, by accident or by design. Before incarnation began, the concept of killing and death was unknown. Once life is terminated on Earth, that concept will once again be impossible to achieve. We concern ourselves, therefore, to those emotions that relate to survival of the individual whilst on Earth.

There is little or no need for those who seek to follow a path towards God to provide nourishment for the ego. Indeed, the opposite obtains. It is similarly unwise for the student to attempt to rid himself of all the emotions that ego forms in his body because he will expose himself to a degree of vulnerability that would cause mayhem in his life and could cause mental breakdown as the full force of the evil emanations swirling round the planet were able to touch his exposed personality and soul. Therefore, initially, it must be obvious that a form of compromise is necessary. We must learn whilst incarnate on Earth to balance the life that we lead with the spiritual life that we would like to lead. Let us state immediately that true spirituality is entirely obtainable whilst on Earth and should that elevated condition be attained, then, by definition, ego would be nonexistent. However, in such a God-fuelled personality, that power of God would envelop the individual in a mighty barrier of spiritual power that nothing would invade. Lesser mortals must be more careful.

It needs also to be said that the chances of any individual achieving true enlightenment whilst on Earth are slim. The forces that play round man, the needs of the body, the requirements of business and domestic life are such that few people have the time, energy, and means of becoming enlightened because that state is not granted by God in a flash, rather like rewarding a faithful dog with a titbit. It is a state that is achieved by long and patient devotion to God. It is a state that is hard won. There are paths that one must walk alone with no one to assist and therefore the state to which we refer is indeed difficult for humans incarnate to achieve. Do not, however, be dismayed. Every inch that you travel each day will remain with you and you will reap the benefit of your efforts when you return to the land of your origin, the spiritual realms.

So, we find that a certain portion of ego remains with most people who follow the path to God. Gradually, over the days and years that you pray, meditate, and serve God, you will find that the negative aspects of personality will diminish. You can afford to lose them. You will be far better without them and you will bring happiness to yourself and to others as you cause them to disappear. Then you will be able to develop those concepts of personality that are positive and helpful to you as they will enable you to relate to your environment, your society, and all the personal relationships with which you deal each day in a positive, peaceful, and relaxed manner.

By allowing negative aspects of ego to die and nurturing positive aspects of personality, you will be maintaining the barrier between your essential attributes that constitute a human and those negative forces that seek to destroy. Such a barrier will be strong but you and your personality will undergo a change, an improvement, as you diminish those negative aspects and increase the positive ones. Once you have developed the positive attributes to a certain degree, however, there will be a reached a point where depression will set in. That depression will be the result of a call sent out by the soul for improvement to be made in the God aspect of the psyche. The soul will send out the call and personality will seek to react by sending out an answering call that confirms that all is well or, in the case under consideration, the personality is unable so to respond and thus turmoil is set up in the emotional content of the individual.

That emotional response will be the cause of depression experienced by the person. That depression will remain for however long it takes for the individual concerned to respond and to take whatever steps are necessary to release and expand within him the God-force that must be set free. The feeling of depression will cause feelings of unhappiness, generally, with the direction that the life of the individual is following and will cause much thought to be expended upon whether one is following the correct course of employment, whether the family environment is correctly established, and, ultimately, what changes can be wrought to bring a feeling of happiness and contentment again to that person.

Until and unless the person so affected satisfies that lacking in personality by taking the necessary steps to develop the spirit of God within himself, the feeling remains. The sense of lacking will remain and will cause trauma within the emotional field of that person and can result in physical illness being experienced in the body that would otherwise have remained healthy. This feeling of depression is the natural result of the soul's awakening or, rather, the spirit of God which has laid dormant within the soul for so long senses that the conditions are now ripe for it to make its appearance. To do so, there must be changes made. The old must be flung away before the new can be installed. So, the spirit of God sets up the conditions to which the personality must respond and that personality can only respond in one of two ways.

Either it is sufficiently endowed with positive attributes as to be able to give an affirmation in which case the changes made will be in line with those positive changes already made within personality or if the call is negative, then those negative aspects must be released in order to fill the void with positive qualities. Should the call be negative, we experience the depression, as was mentioned earlier, which will remain within the personality until the person so affected

132

begins actively to seek God within the peace of his heart. He would do this by the process of prayer, meditation, and service to God.

The law of mutual attraction will bring into his field of experience that which he requires to experience in order to better himself and thus he will gain access to information that will permit him to learn how to pray and to meditate. A suitable arena for service will also be found and he will be encouraged to follow that avenue. He should also strive to bring into his personality attributes that permit the development of mutual attraction of those forces hovering near to him that should they be allowed to become part of his reality will cause soul growth.

It has been mentioned earlier that soul growth is a function of intelligence based on prayer, meditation, and service to God. Whilst that is, in essence, true, it is not the complete story. In order for soul growth to be achieved, it is necessary for a formula of auric conditions to be brought together that will provide suitable conditions for that growth to take place. That formula must be concocted by bringing to the fore suitable situations for the auras so to be manipulated.

For instance, should someone wish to achieve soul growth, then, dependent upon karmic conditions, he would be of a certain sex, age, class, race, etcetera. No two people would be the same and so the formula for everybody would be different. But in the case under consideration, through the effects of those material considerations mentioned, and taking into account all the other factors relevant to that individual since he was conceived, a certain blend of emotions of auric growth patterns would already exist. From that basis, it would be necessary to cause events, auric growth, to occur that would enable that individual to achieve the direction towards perfection that we term soul growth.

Once the decision is reached concerning the direction that advancement must take, it remains to bring into being conditions and events that will permit the desired soul growth to be achieved. Such decisions are not made consciously by the individual. They are far too complex for any Earth-bound personality to make. Wisdom is needed to make such decisions and, of course by implication, the individual seeking soul growth and adjunct to wisdom has not achieved that state. Therefore, the decisions are made for him by the hierarchy of beings that oversee his work and his passage through time.

The decisions, once made, must be put into effect and so the individual would experience changes in his social, business, and domestic life commensurate with the changes required to achieve soul growth. Those changes may be slight or they may be dramatic. They may initially cause happiness or they may cause sadness. It may seem cruel and heartless to state that the elevated souls overseeing each individual would plunge that person into situations of great hardship initially, causing unhappiness and despair but you must remember that those great and wise ones are not interested in the short term nor are they actually interested in childish concepts like happiness, pain, sorrow, joy, etcetera.

Those concepts which seem so important to people of the Earth and indeed are important whilst tied to the Earth have no relevance to greater souls. If the individual wishes to achieve greatness, he must be prepared to suffer to rise to the required heights. An athlete does not become a world-beater by sitting round a fire, warm and snug, with his loved ones. He must be out in all weathers pounding round a track, depriving himself of sweet food and those physical things, considered luxuries, that would bring about his downfall. He must sacrifice all and everything to the desire of becoming great in his field. Similarly, should anyone wish to become great spiritually, they must be prepared to forsake all and follow the path mapped out for them. If it causes hardship initially, then so be it. However, just as a runner as he becomes fit will begin to enjoy running, similarly, the student of God will enjoy his newfound avenues of advancement once he adjusts to them.

It is not the desire that man should suffer in any way. Indeed, the opposite is true. It is the intention of all wise ones to permit all of the Earth access to knowledge that will bring them happiness. However, happiness is not that emotion that can be measured by belly laughs at the expense of others. It is not measured by counting money and securities, nor is it the product of dancing, drinking, and merry making. There is nothing wrong with those things. They have their place amongst people of the Earth and they are intended to bring some light into an otherwise dismal world. But they are childish emotions as are all events and happenings that do not include God awareness. Even the most sophisticated events, an evening at the theatre, ballet, banqueting, etcetera, are childish and the pleasure that they bring is temporary and shallow.

Do not misunderstand our meaning here. Those who become great actors, dancers, and cooks may have made supreme sacrifices during their earthly incarnations to achieve those advancements and, within reason, they will have advanced towards God. We talk, however, of those who dress up and attend such functions. They too, the audience, are necessary. Without them, it would be pointless for the play or the ballet to go on. The food would remain untasted. So, they are important. However, unless they too have studied to appreciate the art being revealed before their eyes, then they do not benefit themselves. They largely waste their time. If they do not understand the art of ballet by firsthand experience, they are not in a position to appreciate the skills being demonstrated. Do not be fooled otherwise.

Critics of the arts often bring acclaim or despondency to performers of art by their criticism. Unless those critics were able to perform at the level of the performers they criticise, their criticisms are invalid. You cannot be an armchair critic. Your statements would have no validity. Any persons who attempted to achieve mastery in any field is urged to ignore the comments of any critic, no matter how highly acclaimed, unless that person is able to rise and demonstrate how it should be done. Ignore those who would tell you otherwise.

Similarly, ignore the teachings in any area of those who are not experts in that area. Life is full of armchair experts. They fool themselves. Do not let them fool you. The pleasure that an audience gains from a concert or a banquet has to be shallow because they have no firsthand knowledge of the difficulties in achieving that which is being portrayed to them. Therefore, they are unable to experience in their hearts the beauty and the skill. Their enjoyment must be shallow and, therefore, it is childish compared to that of the performers.

Only by being expert can you really enjoy anything. To enjoy life, it is necessary to be an expert on life and, to achieve that, it is required that it should be experienced at initially low levels but that those levels should rise until grand mastery is achieved. Only then can one truly appreciate the beauty of life. Do not sit in the armchair wishing you could be a star. You can be great and will be one day. Make that day come closer as you align yourself with the course that destiny decrees you must follow. If it brings you trials and tribulations, then so be it. They will pass as your aura fills with spiritual power and you will arrive at a state of happiness. Do not be afraid. You can do it and you will be helped and coached on every step. Your reward will be great and you will have the happiness, true happiness, of knowing that you are at one with God.

Taking steps to improve one's personality traits by removal of the negative destructive aspects and promoting those more positive attributes would cause change to be wrought throughout the entire body and auras of the person undergoing change. The result of that change would, of course, be an improvement in the personality of that person which will bring light to him and to all who meet him but, whilst those changes are taking effect, there is danger of mental and physical breakdown occurring as voids are created in the energy levels of that person. Those voids will be filled with spiritual energy finally but initially the voids will cause a reduction in physical and emotional energy. Therefore, whilst the student is seeking to improve himself, it is important that he tries to carry out exercises in self-improvement at times when he is able to rest fully and at times when little demand is placed upon him by his employment or his domestic situation. This perforce slows down the rate at which he can achieve improvement but it is better to be slow and thorough rather than chase improvement and finish up damaged physically and psychologically.

The student should constantly monitor his progress and his state of mind and only seek to improve himself whilst he feels fit and well. Should he be prone to mental stress, he will recognise the signs soon enough and must cease to meditate and criticise himself forthwith until his body informs him that he may once again continue.

The mind should be considered rather like a muscle in the body. A muscle may be trained through steady exercise to perform great feats but, once strained, the muscle is torn and may never be capable again of the same feats. If you permit your mind to become strained resulting in nervous breakdown, it ,too, will never be capable of quiet the same feats. There will always remain a tendency towards breakdown.

Therefore, nurture yourself. Do not permit any excesses in your life either spiritual or temporal and you will become stronger and more capable of doing God's work. God needs capable workers, not an army of cripples. Ensure that you are able to play your part to the best of your ability. God will appreciate that you are not a machine and require rest from time to time. If and when you do rest and take a break from your spiritual development and activities, inform your colleagues of your intentions and inform your spiritual advisors also. Then, rest without thought for man or God.

So often, the novice feels the need for spiritual rest and yet feels guilty about taking it. Therefore, he tries to rest and yet, because he does not relax, he becomes more tired and strained than he was before. Do not feel guilty about rest. You will need rest from time to time and you have a duty to refresh yourself fully in order to return to the fray able to work. Therefore, when you feel the need to relax, do so. Sleep all you need. Seek fresh air and the peace of the countryside. Do all that you can to relax and you will quickly become rejuvenated. After that, you will look forward once again to taking up the struggle to perfect yourself. You will be acting correctly and in the way that nature would act. Even trees, mighty and powerful things, rest in the winter. Make sure that you rest when you feel the need.

Having achieved a measure of success in ridding oneself of the thoughts that we acquire upon arrival on Earth, it will be noticed that the friends that we had may start to disappear from our social circle and new friends will come into the circle. This is inevitable. Under the law of mutual attraction, like attracts like, and as our personality changes, so we would change our circle of friends. Should we continue to develop spiritually, then we will continue to change. Therefore, our circle of friends will change again and again. This must and will happen and nothing can prevent it from so happening.

From that, one can see that it is pointless in forming too close a relationship with any person. This statement needs explaining. One can appreciate that our work colleagues and those whom we meet during our daily round have amongst them numbers of people who will be at different levels of spiritual advancement. So, from that group, certain ones will be drawn towards each person. However, as we advance spiritually, so those relationships will become strained and other people will be attracted to the student. This will cause resentment amongst the first group who will feel rejected. In a work situation, an office, or a factory, where one is forced to work in close proximity with those who now feel rejected, this situation can cause pressure. Such pressure is not wanted. Life, spiritual life, is difficult enough without the backbiting caused by simple souls who do not understand the events occurring within and around them. Therefore, it is better not to form a too close relationship with one's colleagues and friends.

View those relationships as temporary even though you may work side by side with those people for many years. Do not be snobbish or standoffish. Just be natural and be friendly but do not try to form close relationships with them. However, your family and family relations are different. If you are married, you have a duty to try to love your partner. You do not have the right to change your spouse. So, as you advance and he or she does not, there is a tendency to grow apart. Do not allow this to happen. Use your increased spirituality to provide you with the humility to mask your spiritual superiority and to allow love to remain at all costs. There is nothing worse than a spiritual snob and even though you may make great strides, you will be low indeed compared to the advances that can be achieved. Recognise this and use your spirituality to provide you with the simplicity that you must develop anyway on day. Ensure that your spouse does not sense your greatness. That will indeed be a measure of your greatness. If you can spend your life in true love with a partner who is less spiritually advanced than you, then you will truly be advanced.

The same applies to your attitudes to your sons and daughters and to those who are close to you. Love them all in purity, accepting them as they are. Do not try to change them. It is inevitable that change will take place within the personality of those around you as you improve your personality. Such change may, however, come slowly into being and, therefore, you must wait patiently and expectantly until your spouse and family responds to the benign waves emitted from your aura and to grow in stature. Then you may begin to live as a happy family.

Since the time that man first incarnated on Earth, he has been held in the grip of numerous forces originating in the minds of the creatures of the Earth and in the mind concept of the Earth itself for, make no mistake, the planet Earth, like all things is alive as an entity just as you are, and just as you have a mind and ego, etcetera, so the Earth has the same attributes. The scale is different, the degree of consciousness is different, but basically all things created having life within them have a degree of vivacity. To live requires a form of mind. Do not suppose that you have to be human to be endowed with a mind. That Earth mind permits forms of feelings, of emotions, far removed from our concepts to swirl around its surface and within its body. You can imagine that any emotional reflexes created by the mind of the planet Earth would be basic in nature and would be the last sort of emotion to be needed for assimilation into the human condition. And yet, from the day of our birth to the day of our death, those emotions swirl around us, forming ever greater bonds between us and the Earth.

This matter was mentioned in an earlier chapter and, as was further mentioned, the state of being trapped and tied to the Earth will continue for the duration of the Earthly incarnation unless steps are taken to rise above it. The steps to be taken, the action required to develop the spirit within the individual is always and ever the same. Prayer, meditation, and devotion to God will free one from the grip of the Earth and from the grip of, indeed, any base or maligned force, liberating the individual to live at peace with himself and with his fellow man. A person with spiritual attributes is perforce a creature of peace, beauty, and happiness, and, by the nature of the forces operating in the universe, everybody that he comes into contact with will also benefit. It has been stated that the measure of one's advancement is not the degree in which one loves but is the degree that one is loved by others. This statement is, in essence, true. Certainly, should one be advanced and by the same token happy, then contact with others will bring happiness into their lives and so the advanced ones will be liked.

However, it is also true that people of the Earth sense the presence of an advanced soul and will react with anger, hatred, and hostility to that person. That situation is dangerous to the student as he advances in spirituality. It is dangerous in the sense that he could suffer emotional and mental abuse. He could suffer physical abuse. Therefore, the student is advised to tell no one about his interest in God, and the spiritual path, until he's sure of that person and persuaded that he is sufficiently advanced so as not to be a danger to the student. Of course, everybody that the student encounters will, through the auras, sense to a degree the spirituality of the student but, fortunately, those whose souls sleep will be unable to read the information from their auras with clarity and, therefore, will not fully appreciate the level from which the student operates. Should that student declare verbally his commitment to God, then of course the first individual will immediately and without conscious realisation put into action the steps to dishonour the student. Although a person of the Earth cannot do any real harm to a disciple of God once you realise that physical death does not constitute harm, then it is obvious that the disciple has nothing to fear.

But life is difficult enough without becoming involved with those committed to the downfall of the student. The advice is to leave those whose souls sleep, sleeping still, and follow God in peace, in love, and to keep one's own counsel. You will know soon enough when you have made the acquaintance of like-minded individuals to you. Nurture their friendship and ignore everybody else. Learn to go through your daily round interacting with your work colleagues and those whom you meet, indulging in chit chat about the weather, politics, etcetera, and never mention your main interest – namely, God. It is difficult to do initially but with practice it can be achieved and it will save you much aggravation.

From that standpoint, it is also possible to work in the daily round whilst inwardly meditating on God. This does not imply that one daydreams nor does it suggest that one should limit one's concentration in the work being undertaken. It is a strange role for the mind to play in being split so that one part is concentrating entirely on the work being performed whilst, at the same time, another part of the brain is concentrating on God. It perhaps seems impossible but it can be done.

The state mentioned has been sought after and achieved by many involved with various activities throughout time and throughout the planet. Workers performing fairly intricate, but nevertheless repetitive, tasks learn to allow their fingers to perform the required tasks while their minds wander along daydream paths or the individual chats to a neighbour at the next work position. Monks, too, learn to concentrate on their daily round, performing it expertly and with dedication whilst at the same time occupying their minds with a mantra or prayer to God repeated endlessly.

Therein lies a clue for others who would wish to learn the skill of splitting the mind successfully in two. The student could consider reciting, silently in his mind, a repetitive prayer to God. He will find, should he try to keep it up, that his attention will begin to wander initially and he will not be able to hold the prayer in his attention whilst operating at a different level during his Earthly tasks. However, should he persevere, he will gradually be able to achieve a state where he will be able to perform the tasks that duty compels whilst carrying out meditation without thinking about that meditation. That state also is not the required one. Perseverance will ultimately bring him into a condition where he will be able consciously to perform his duties on Earth whilst, at the same time, praying or meditating or discussing matters of interest with his companions in the afterlife. This state is very valuable to achieve and it must be said that very few people indeed have been able to completely achieve it. It is not the end, however. It is possible to go on indefinitely, learning to split the mind into evermore segments, each one acting independently of the other.

History has recorded that some people have been tested and proved to be capable of completing more than twenty different tasks concurrently. This is all very well but we are not interested in fairground feats. We are concerned with the development of body, mind, and soul in a trinity unto unity towards God. It will suffice if the student can learn to perform two tasks at once. Then he will be in a position of serving God and mammon, both at the same time. This state will be valuable because it is important to work and to serve mankind. All too often nowadays, people are discouraged from working because, due to economic features and conditions created by business and government, the numbers of workers required round the world is decreasing whilst the population of the world is generally increasing. This results in a climate where unemployment is accepted as a way of life.

This state of affairs is devilish because human beings need to serve. They need to serve God. God manifests Himself in things and in living beings like man. By serving his fellow man, by interacting, and by relationships often unpleasant, a person may advance greatly towards perfection. Idleness, even when commissioned and sanctified by government, causes man to reject his opportunity to serve and so to advance. Therefore, the student is instructed to find some form of employment. Prayer to God will rapidly bring to his preview the necessary vacancy and he should accept it and perform his duties to the best of his abilities. It is important, also, to avoid idleness because that condition can cause the spirit of God latent in man, yet always alert and ready to burst forth, to push man into areas of discontentment where he might turn to drink, to gambling, or to crime to satisfy the urges of his soul. Doing a useful job at work for his fellow travellers through time will ensure that the spirit of God remains satisfied and so he too will remain satisfied.

Now we need to concern ourseves with an aspect of personality which is often overlooked and yet which, when brought into the light for examination, will help us to understand ourselves a great deal better than we presently do. We refer to that aspect called intelligence. Why do we imply that intelligence is overlooked when scores in colleges, universities, and institutes all over the world are directing their energies to the development of nothing else?

The answer is simple. Every educational establishment throughout the annals of civilisation have tried to develop knowledge in the mistaken idea that knowledge equates with intelligence. It is not true. Any person willing to devote himself to the pursuit can enrol at a college or at a university and study. Providing that he has a retentive memory and providing that he devotes sufficient time in amassing a plethora of information, he will pass his examinations. He will be able to rise to great heights from an academic point of view. He might become a doctor of divinity or a doctor of medicine or, yet again, a doctor of philosophy. However, at no point does he require intelligence.

Even intelligence tests are merely aimed to those who have met a similar or identical problem before and therefore trot out the answers to the amazement of those who have never seen such a problem. Intelligence, by definition, implies that a person is able to make cognitive leaps from that which he knows to that which he does not know but recognises, by some deep factor within him, is true. One can see from that, that the more information a person has, generally, the more he is able to consider in order to assist him in leaping into the unknown. But, nevertheless, most people, when required to make that cognitive leap, would flounder.

However, intelligence is a gift of the spirit and it can be developed. Like all gifts of the spirit, the development is simple in that all it requires is prayer, meditation, and devotion to God but, like all of the gifts of the spirit, it takes long years in order to develop it. It is a state akin to wisdom. Wisdom is a state that can be described as merging the higher godly states with the lower Earthly states but also requires intelligence before wisdom can be truly achieved.

140

Many people are of the opinion that intelligence is formed at birth by genetic makeup. That implies that the parents of a child, should they have a measure of intelligence, then that child, too, will be similarly gifted. The offspring of teachers, for example, often achieve well academically although what they achieve in their future domestic lives is less often than perfect. The truth is, of course, that, for a start, the offspring of an academic couple would possibly be an individual who by the law of mutual attraction would already have developed a degree of the quality under consideration. Secondly, surrounded by an environment where learning and study were the norm, it is inevitable that the child will follow suit and amass information far in advance of his peer students. He would, therefore, find passing examinations easy.

However, as was mentioned before, if we follow such precocious children into adulthood, we find all too often that once they are forced out of a cloistered academic environment and into the real world, they are often at sea. They may make poor businessmen, having little business acumen, or their personal relationship with the opposite sex, or their own sex for that matter, may prove disastrous. And so we see that knowledge, whilst very important, is not intelligence. That condition implies that the individual, whatever situation he may find himself in, would quickly assess the situation and be able to make the right decisions in order to fit in with whatever state or condition was presented. It implies that his relationship with all life, with all people, including his spouse, would be a reflection of the beauty that ideology dictates it should be.

That condition is far removed from book learning. It is far removed from deep knowledge about any subject. It is a state where learning leaves off and the individual is able to advance on his own, following a path that he cannot see and yet he knows is there towards the goal and he will, and does, realise when he has achieved that goal. It is a gift of the spirit achieved through the trinity of prayer, meditation, and service to God. It is available to all. Should you wish to become intelligent yourself, then follow the path. Without intelligence, you cannot achieve wisdom and without wisdom you cannot be free of the Earth and at one with God and with all the liberated souls that there are in God's kingdom waiting to welcome you to their noble ranks.

By applying yourself as was mentioned above, one by one the gifts will be granted to you. Indeed, they are already within you, latent. They are hidden by ego. As ego disappears and God-filled purity replaces it, so the gifts come into being. Seek them with avidity. They will bring joy and blessings to you and to all mankind. Seek and ye shall find. Knock and it shall be opened unto you. Ask and it shall be given unto you. It is your duty to yourself and to God to do so, so let it be.

Let us now consider an aspect of personality which it is joyous indeed to consider. It is that which relates to the seeking of pleasure in all its various forms, from the sordid lusts of a degenerate to the joy of angels singing in Heaven in praise of the Lord. It gives us joy to discuss such matters because, all too often, we have had to implore you to accept advice which implies sacrifice and suffering in order to advance. The subject of pleasure, of joy, of laughter, and of happiness is a state different indeed from the others previously discussed because we do not need to ask you to suffer today in order to reap the benefits tomorrow. We ask you to relax and enjoy the fruits of your labours past.

We know that pleasure takes many forms. Have you ever watched a cat who has caught a mouse and is playing with it? The cat is not hungry or else it would kill and eat it in an instant and so it holds the mouse in its mouth and then lets it go. The poor, terrified mouse runs away. Just when it thinks that it is free, the cat lunges and holds it with its paws to repeat the exercise again and again until the poor mouse, either through fear, exhaustion, or damage, expires, after which the cat will probably lose interest in it and walk away to sleep the rest of the day well-pleased with itself. It is obvious to the onlooker that the cat derives pleasure from such an act which, in our eyes, is completely wrong and would incur great penalty in karmic terms should we similarly indulge ourselves. Why should it do such a thing and why does it gain pleasure?

One may state, first of all, that it is natural in the world for cats to catch mice. They are carnivorous animals and live by such acts. However, a marauding feline would spot his quarry, creep up, and pounce. He would then quickly bite the neck of his prey to kill it and would swallow it whole in a few moments. The act of eating is pleasurable for all creatures as it is for man. Therefore, we can understand why it enjoys its meal. But, more than that, the act of hunting becomes pleasurable because it is associated with eating. It is associated with the fulfillment of the drive within an animal to provide itself with food in order that the spirit within that animal should have an opportunity to express itself through that animal. The spirit being satisfied, the animal is satisfied.

Satisfaction brings happiness, therefore, the act of hunting quickly becomes associated with happiness. Even if the cat is fully fed by a caring owner, the cat still seeks the satisfaction gained from hunting. Should he come across a mouse, then of course he goes through the act of hunting it again and again until the mouse is dead. At that point, happiness ceases for the cat. He is not desirous to eat it, preferring the tasty food provided by his human servant. So he leaves the mouse and turns elsewhere.

One can see immediately from that that our noble lords dressed in their hunting pinks or armed with guns costing a king's ransom are acting very much like the cat as they charge over the countryside in pursuit of the fox or blast defenceless pheasants from the sky. It is the act of hunting associated with the act of eating that gives them that satisfaction. They cannot eat all day but rather than to eat and to turn their attention to more useful pastimes, they perform the act of hunting again and again as they destroy drove after drove of beautiful creatures in order to give themselves happiness.

Should one point out to such a person that he is acting in an animalistic fashion, he would possibly raise an eyebrow. The act of hunting is made respectable because it is raised into an art form. Special clothing is manufactured in order to provide the uniform that corresponds to the state of mind. The weapons used are honed and polished until they are things of terrible beauty. No expense is spared to achieve the best possible conditions for gratification of the senses but, of course, the student of higher things will recognise immediately that such people are at one with the animal kingdom. Their souls sleep still and they are scarcely human in the terms that we consider. Strange, isn't it, that all too often those who hunt are the rich, the influential, the leaders of our world, and, even more often, the kings and sovereigns of countries?

However, that is not to say that many more humble people are saints. The poor hunt with dogs, with ferrets, or they go fishing. Such pleasure as they find, sad to say, is at a price. We know that the law of karma will bring the retribution of an eye for an eye and a tooth for a tooth to them. We do not imply that they must be shot or ripped apart by dogs as many times as they killed birds and foxes. No. We mean that the suffering that they've inflicted on God's kingdom in order to gain a perverted form of pleasure will ultimately have to be paid off in this life, in the afterlife or, possibly, by reincarnating in miserable conditions again and again.

It is clear from the above that pleasure to us implies that it must be harmless to others. This requires some study in order to quantify and qualify. We have a large gamut of experiences which bring us pleasure. We will not discuss the degrading spectacle of people who gain satisfaction from torturing humans or animals nor those who rape defenceless women or who perform unnatural acts against people against their will. Such acts will bring a price, a burden of karma, which will take a long time to pay.

We do, however, regard sex acts between consenting adults as bringing pleasure. Once again, it is an animal attribute but it is harmless. It brings happiness to humans and to animals because it is important that copulation is carried out that the species might continue. The student is referred to the chapter "Dictates Of The Heart" for an at-length discussion on the attributes of the sex act and its relation to the spiritual path. We merely state at this point that, providing both partners consent, then that act brings joy and indeed a certain and important psychological effect which helps balance the personalities of both parties. This is good and prevents a person from becoming neurotic, a condition all too often found in those who pass their lives and still remain virgin.

From that, we consider laughter. It is not very often that humour lends itself to innocent pleasure because it is almost a tradition that comedians gain applause from an audience by mocking people, situations, and events, and, therefore, such laughter that comes spontaneously from the audience is hardly innocent. Indeed, all too often, those who are the butt of the jokes take deep exception to being laughed at. It must also be stated that it is not very kind to gain pleasure from contemplating a person slipping on a banana skin. So why is it that traditional theatre, films, and plays often portray sad events and encourage the audience to laugh? Is such humour innocent and should one permit oneself the freedom to be amused by such humour?

Animals, it must be noted, have no sense of humour. Laughter is not part of animal makeup. Their happiness is gained in other respects, in being part of a pack, in having a warm dry layer, in eating, etcetera. They do not seek further than those basic needs. We realise, then, that laughter and humour must be part of the spiritual makeup of man. It is a godly concept and therefore should be innocent, harming and offending no one. What sort of humour, which events, can we laugh at without causing offence to any other person?

Let us state immediately that traditional humour will be dropped from your reality one day. It is usually very childish and it is usually used as a safety valve to release tension caused by deep-rooted fears and phobias. That is why humour is considered to be very close to tragedy. We laugh at someone slipping on a banana skin because we are glad that it was not us. We laugh when a clown receives a custard pie in the face because we know that that is one custard pie that we will not receive in our faces. This state of mind is a result of being a victim of the Earth. The planet Earth is a hard place to live on. It is termed the school of hard knocks. It does not have to be. Once the soul awakens within an individual and once, through prayer, meditation, and devotion to God, the auras fill with power, then that person will be free of the Earth. It will no longer have any hold over him and any harm or trouble that comes his way can be deflected by the mighty shield of the power of God.

To those whose souls still sleep, of course, such information is dismissed as being nonsense and so they go on their way constantly in fear of what terrible event will befall them next. No wonder they seek escapism in watching other people suffer, even in a theatrical sense. For such people, of course, the humour portrayed nightly on television, on stage, and on film is valid and it is a useful escape valve for them. To those who have entered a wider concept of life, to the student on the path to God, he will quickly see how pointless such humour is because, to him, he has no need of an escape valve. He is not dogged by fears and phobias. He knows that nothing can harm him and all that try will fail.

Therefore, he turns to a different form of humour. He laughs at different events. That which the student will find to bring joy is that which fills his soul with beauty at the wonder of power of God. He may sit in a garden and watch a fountain playing over rocks in the bright sunshine. He may watch the water droplets as they shimmer and scintillate with the many colours that sunlight consists of. As he gazes at that scene of beauty, his concentration will become so intense that he will forget all else and identify with the sense of beauty being revealed before his eyes and for his delight. That beauty will cause his heart to sing with joy and he may well find himself laughing spontaneously for no better reason than he's supremely happy and wishes to express that happiness.

Similarly, he may watch animals playing in a field – lambs, for instance. Their antics, as they leap and jump to express the energy of the spirit within them, is surely one of the great joys of spring. Study those lambs. Identify with the simple joy that they feel and you too will be filled with joy. After such simple and harmless pursuits, who would need to seek gratification in imagining someone falling over or someone making fun at his mother-in-law?

If you are still at the stage where you gain some happiness from scenarios that use people in some unhappy or unfortunate situation, and wish to rise above it, pray for guidance. Limit the amount of time that you spend in indulging or watching such humour and try to gain joy from less harmful observations. Gradually, you will begin to see the beauty of the simple God-created things in life and your desire to seek gratification at the expense of others will cease.

It may seem strange to consider that one can train one's personality to advance and decline in specific areas rather as if the personality were separate from the being who is able to manipulate it.  It suggests that there are two people in one inside every human being. It has been noted that the person who looks out at the world from behind the mask, the persona, is in some way separate and individual from the body which stumbles along through life, making mistakes and, all too often, causing pain to himself and to others. Many learned people have noted this peculiar fact and have commented on it, often with great skill and insight. However, for the student on the path to God, it is not easy to acquire relevant information about the duality of personality as the tomes produced by psychologists tend to be rather weighty, almost as if verbosity equated with veracity.

So, we will explain in a few short lines some of the aspects of personality, its apparent duality, and, much more importantly, how to combine the individual aspects into a unit firmly based on God. Initially, a person destined to be born on Earth has needs to mould round his spirit of God contained within the soul a number of bodies of light that we term auras. Those auras, as has been explained earlier, are actually a part of the individual and are as real within their sphere of manifestation as the human body is on the Earth plane. However, just as with the physical body, the auras have no particular power in themselves. Without the spirit animating the body, it becomes a lifeless corpse.  Similarly, a spirit of the individual in combination with the power emanating from the Great Spirit, God, will be able to create potential within the auras for development by that person. Should the person concerned have the knowledge, desire, and awareness, he may fill those auras with spiritual power rather as a deep-sea diver fills his underwater suit with compressed air. As the auras fill, they become strong, viable bodies themselves, attached to the psyche of the person under consideration and are an integral part of that person but they are only bodies, vehicles, and, like all vehicles, they require a driver in order that they may fulfill their function.

The driver is, of course, not the body. The driver is a life force within the body. It is not the spirit of God. That spirit is the animating force, the fuel used to drive the vehicle but that fuel and the driver are separate from each other. Therefore, we repeat that the spirit of God within you is not you. That you is the person who looks back at you from a mirror. What, then, is this mysterious person called you? Clearly, it is not the personality. As was stated earlier, the personality is an aspect created by you often in conjunction with higher beings who guide and protect you in order that you can relate to the path that you have chosen to follow. It is a means of relating to that path and also a protective armour that ensures that you are able to parry attacks on all planes.

Next, what is ego? In our terminology, ego is part of personality. It is the driving force that makes you feel separate from all other people and from all other things. It helps you to survive by giving you the drive to survive. Therefore, we have briefly covered most aspects of a human being. We looked at and discounted the spirit, the body, the auras, the personality, and the ego. Still, we have not discovered who you are. Clearly, you are none of these because you can manipulate most of them, lose many of them, and still you remain as the controlling force behind them all. We, therefore, state that the source of that sense of being, the true you behind the mask, is something that we will term the id.

That strange term used and misused by psychologists and by those investigating the mind behind matter is suitable to identify the force that is essentially you. The place of the id within the context of the overall personality and life forces, is that it is separate from them all. As was stated earlier, the directors of life, when creating human beings, take a portion of life force and implant it with certain instructions that will cause it to attract matter destined for humanity. That life force, then, slowly descends and evolves, advances and grows, until it becomes a fully-fledged human being, but the spirit of God, the essence of all life, wonderful though it is, is not able to think for itself. It is, and we must apologise for the use of the word, merely a life force. Something must direct all that is into a cohesive whole. Therefore, by the power of the law of mutual attraction, as matter is drawn round the nucleus of the spirit of God, a strange event happens.

That matter forms a gestalt which has been described as the "whole being greater than the sum of the parts". This gestalt is the source of the creation of an identity, the id. It is realised that such a concept is difficult to grasp but, nevertheless, it is so. The even more strange fact is that everybody's id is identical. All people are initially like identical twins in that the ids of all human beings have one sense of identity. Later on, as groups of beings combine, then, a group id is formed and so on, but the individual id of you, me, and of everybody else, whilst being identical in all respects, realises that, in order to follow a path through life, a sense of separateness from all other humans is initially necessary.

So, the id creates personality and ego and a more recognisable form of human comes into being. As we follow the path back towards God, as has been mentioned, the personality and ego will gradually shrivel and die and one finds that the sense of separateness is declining as one realises the identity that is between all ids. Later on still, as perfection is continued to be sought, the ids join into closer harmony and at some stage, the individual ids will be dropped and those people would now no longer consider themselves to be separate beings but would merge into a group. A group id then takes over and, later still, the groups will join into larger groups, etcetera.

However, that is a long way into the future for all of us. We will not confuse you at this point by entering into comment about the fine nuances of life. It is sufficient, at this stage, for the student to realise that he has a personal identity and id which, through personality and ego, appears to make him separate from all else but that, behind it all, his personal identity is at one with the personal identity of all beings who will ever live, are living, and who have gone before. It is only personality and ego that causes the sense of separateness. They perform a useful function at the moment.

Eventually, the great day will dawn when they can be dropped and a much larger state, a more happier condition, can be entered into. Do not try to rush that day. You will fail. Modify the personality that you have, starving negative aspects out of all existence and nurturing the positive ones, and you will be amply rewarded.

# CHAPTER 13 - THINGS THAT ARE TO BE

Can you imagine a situation in which the past, the present, and the future were all one, all related into a continuous stream in which the only aspect that was relevant was sequence of events? No? Then you are probably wise. It is almost impossible for a person incarnate on Earth and tied to concepts of time, of calendar, of lunar events to appreciate that time, in fact, does not exist and it is possible, indeed probable, that even after we have carefully explained the facts, that many of you will reject those facts as not being an accurate portrayal of reality. However, we will do our best to present to you the information in a readily understandable fashion and leave the rest to your credulity.

We live in a world that is governed by clocks. Those clocks, assuming that they are working correctly, give an indication of the passing moments related to the rotation of the Earth. It is deduced that morning sunrise appears with great regularity. If one lived on the equator then, indeed, sunrise would be at a particular time each day and sunset would follow exactly 12 hours later. This state of measuring the passage of time and to chronicle this passage has been of great use in the development of mankind and it is true to say that the development of civilisation would have taken a different course had timekeeping not been invented.

Whether that latent alternative development would have been better or worse is another matter. Certainly, it would have been different. However, man has recently discovered that the rules governing his ability to observe the passage of time do not nearly cover events as they occur in nature. His ability to keep grasp upon time is very tenuous indeed. He has observed that movement destroys that time-keeping accuracy. Fortunately, the speed at which man travels over the surface of the planet is comparatively leisurely and so the difference measured between clocks stationary on the surface of that planet and clocks travelling over it is minimal. Once man begins to travel faster, of course, the difference becomes more marked until it is virtually meaningless.

It has been supposed that if one travelled at the speed of light, time would cease to be of relevance. In fact, we state to you that, in real terms in relation to cosmic consciousness, time has never existed. We are interested in quantifying laws that exist generally, not within a limited and finite set of circumstances, and we know that the rules concerning time on Earth, though important to the type of civilisation developed, nevertheless, are meaningless. We state again that time does not exist. However, sequence of events does.

A mayfly is born, grows to maturity, mates, and dies in a short space of time as measured on Earth. Nevertheless, it completes its life cycle. An elephant does the same as does a tortoise or a whale. Those creatures may take many years in earthly terms to complete their life cycles but each one goes through the same motions. Is the life of an elephant more important than a mayfly, as it takes longer to achieve its potential? No. Each and everything is as important as everything else. Therefore, the mayfly and the elephant perform the same function in God's eyes. The difference in time scale is immaterial. It is the fact that they live that is important and that they procreate. It is the sequence of events that are real, not the time scale.

From that, we observe all too often people become bogged down in their minds with the amount of time that is spent producing an object. How many objects can be produced in any given period of time and ultimately the financial profit to be derived from such events? This way of life is based on a number of wrong suppositions and on wrong criteria. In the first place, as was mentioned, time itself does not exist. Therefore, the concept of hourly wage, for example, is wrong. The concept of time and motion study is wrong. It is the inevitable result of a mistaken sense of separateness from God.

If one truly had faith that God would provide, it would be possible to produce articles not for profit but for the benefit of fellow man. Those articles, if distributed amongst people for the benefit of those people and to the glory of God, would be rewarded by God and the manufacturer would be rewarded by the power of God. If you do not believe it to be so then you would fail if you tried. If you have the confidence in God so as to be able to place yourself in His hands, then try it. You will be amazed that it does in fact work. God will protect and nurture His own. You can work for the benefit of the power of God manifest in man and you will be rewarded by God. You will want for nothing. Faith is all that is necessary.

Therefore, we now have two aspects to our life outside of time: sequence of events and faith in God. To that we add a third. It is normal amongst business people to pay great heed to the amount of energy expended in producing an article not because the businessmen are philanthropic enough to care about the well-being of their workers but because energy costs money. Money spent implies reduced profit. Businesses thrive on profit. We say to you, take no regard for the amount of energy that you expend personally on completing a project for God. However, do not waste resources.

If you expend a great deal of your own energy upon any work, you will find that that energy will be replaced, and more, by God, providing that the work was performed for the Glory of God. But, you are asked to pay great heed to the natural resources being used around you. Gas, electricity, oil – all these things are the result of processes occurring within the Earth and, because they are exploited for profit, are not replaced. Therefore, use them sparingly.

Now let us assemble the whole trinity of sequence of events, of faith in God, and of energy expended. What has this strange concoction of apparently unrelated events got to do with time, the past, or the future? If a workman uses his energy to create something to the glory of God in the sure knowledge that he will be rewarded by God and considers not how much effort he personally expends, he

150

will find that the work that he achieves will be beautiful and will transcend the limitations of the throwaway society in which we now live. His work will go on into the future and will be admired by future generations. That will be the link with him over the years almost as if a hand was being stretched out in both directions to join the past with the future.

It is not necessary, however, to manufacture something in order to reach out in time. If you think about it, the manufactured article is an extension of the person's mind and that mind is the creating force. It is possible for someone to train their mind to reach out in all directions in an endeavour to join with and be at one with the minds of others. With training, the mind is capable of performing extraordinary tasks and moving backwards and forwards is one of them. The methodology of performing such feats, as usual, is quite simple. It is the inevitable process of prayer, meditation, and service to God that will allow the necessary aura to expand with power and that is the key to reaching outside of the present.

Let us assume that the required degree of development has been achieved. Then, the student will be able to reach out and explore those realms of the past and of the future. The past is fixed, or nearly so, and so exploration of it should be fairly easy and yield consistent results. What he observes, however, depends upon a great deal of things. To give an example, let us imagine that you are in a spaceship and that you are visiting Earth from a distant planet, say, Mars. Let us also imagine that the captain of the spaceship decides to drop several of you, the crew, off towards the planet Earth at various points and at different moments. What would you all report back?

One of you lands upon a polar icecap. He reports back that the Earth is covered in ice. Another lands in a hot desert. He reports back that the planet is covered in sand and is baking hot. Another lands in the sea, another in a city. Some land during the daytime and some at night. From the massive conflicting evidence returned to the captain by the scouts, the poor captain would be justified in concluding that the planet Earth was a place capable of turning his scouts mad and yet each was telling the truth.

Should you learn to enter with your mind that area where records of events are stored, the akashic, what would you see? Would that which you see bear any semblance to reality? How could you decipher the truth from your observations? The answer, of course, is to proceed with caution, observing all and refraining from making decisions concerning the veracity of your observations. It is obvious that that which is observed is dependent upon the viewpoint of the observer. The observation is further coloured by the personality of the observer and, lastly, that which is seen could possibly be a figment of the imagination. The last aspect is the most difficult to deal with because it requires that the student acts in a dispassionate manner, putting aside any wants, hopes, or fears so that he does not inter-react with the event being portrayed to him. Should he unconsciously use his imagination to create a vista then he will be the last to realise it. It will appear real to him, as real as any genuine experience.

Therefore, it has been stated that astral travel or any technique related to it should only be taken by those whose feet are firmly on the ground, metaphorically speaking. Imagination is a useful gift for creating works of fiction or for use as a drawing board to plan a future creation but it is not based on reality. Therefore, for the serious student who wishes to pursue a path through the akashic record, he must learn to prevent his imagination from contributing images. Should he succeed in so doing then that which is observed must be real, no matter how bizarre it may seem. However, it may be of no use to the student to examine, for example, a barren wasteland when he may be interested in meeting people in order to gain points of view. Nor would it serve any purpose to investigate a sub-aqua situation when the action that he is interested in is taking place on dry land.

So, the student must learn to direct his thoughts towards the areas of akashic record that he does wish to investigate and to disregard any other images observed en route. The technique is, in essential, simple. He merely directs his mind to go to that area and to hold his attention fixed until he does. That may seem simple enough until you realise that that is what a darts player does. He fixes his desire on aiming for a bull's eye, for example, but how many darts does he have to throw before he can hit the bull's eye every time? You will find exactly the same problem when you first begin to enter the akashic record area. Perseverance will, however, bring results. What will you find when you are able to examine those records?

Every event that has ever happened throughout the annals of earthly existence relating to mankind are there and are available for inspection. Each planet has round it its own akashic area so that should you wish to examine the record relating to events on Mars or Venus, for example, you could, with training, do so. Interpretation of the viewed events would, however, be difficult to achieve meaningfully. Events close to Earth are more easily made sense of. Therefore, you could view the great battles of the world, the life of Jesus, or a peasant going about his daily chores. Whatever you wish to view, you may.

Further, you may interact with those records. Although the images of the past are fixed and finished with, you may take a portion of them and, by using your imagination in a controlled fashion, you may take part in the events occurring. You could, for example, go with Hannibal over the Alps leading an elephant or you could help a great surgeon perform an operation. There are no limits to that which you can do in this area, only the limits that you place upon yourself. You can see from the above that you could learn a great deal of value through you.

152

Who would not like to return to the time of Jesus and listen to him speak and watch him perform miracles? Who would not like to break bread with the master? You can experience the wonder and the power of his God-fuelled personality. It will act as a source of great inspiration to you throughout your life. This wonderful area is there to be examined by you if you will take the effort, first of all, to enter it and then to control your path through it. If you are unwilling so to do then it remains closed to you.

Having considered the past, what of the future? Many people are of the opinion that the future, as it is yet to come, cannot possibly exist. To a certain extent, they are right. The past is fixed and finished with and nothing can alter it but the future is much more fluid. You may, perhaps, read another page of this book or you may go for a walk. You may take a bath or play a game of football. There are apparently endless possible number of events that can occur. That is, in fact, not true.

Let us state immediately that accidents do occur and that they are unpredictable in the sense that one cannot tell exactly when one may occur. Let us take an example that one hopes will not occur. The chair that you are sitting on may have a fault. It could be suggested that inspection would reveal that fault and remedial action could be taken. However, we will assume that the fault is ignored. At some stage, then, the chair will collapse. Who could tell exactly when it will collapse? If it were possible to so predict then one could rise from the chair seconds before it crashes to the ground and possible harm to the person could be prevented. It is not possible to know with exactitude such a thing and so the chair collapses eventually and the person unlucky enough to be sitting in it suffers a bruised body and dignity!

Similarly, with regard to health, one should look after the body but, assuming that one does not, then an illness of some sort may strike without warning, perhaps fatally. Although that illness could have been prevented, the exact moment when it strikes is unknown. That is fact. Many religions, typically Eastern ones, have a fatalistic attitude to accidents, stating that it is the will of God that such things should happen and ascribe to God the dreadful responsibility of making them occur at a precise moment. God does not operate in that fashion. Accidents occur in a random fashion and are unpredictable. They are not altogether unpreventable, however. Remedial or preventive measures with regard to personal health, the lifestyle, and the objects one uses is effective. Prayer too, for protection, will put a shield of armour round a person to prevent accidents occurring. But still, sometimes, things do go wrong and, indeed, sometimes happy events accidentally occur. There is always a random element in life.

Ignoring accidents for a moment, the possible future of any individual is, to a certain extent, mapped out for that individual long before he incarnated on Earth. That person, in conjunction with his guides and advisors, would have decided upon a course of events and actions that were necessary for the development of that person. The aim is to bring the individual to God awareness but the route decided upon may be long and tedious. The route planned would, of course, not be a random one but would be designed to complement the areas of personality of the individual that lacked perfection. Then, by the law of mutual attraction, the person who draws certain events towards him actually draws the future unconsciously towards him.

Because he is unaware of that future and the areas that require treatment, he may try to stray from the path and into areas that might appear attractive to him. He would meet a dead end on any such path. With gentleness or with violence, the law of mutual attraction would draw him back onto the path that must be walked. Thus, you see, there is indeed a very limited number of variations to the future that lies before a person. Try as he might, he is compelled to walk the path. However, although the path is, in broad terms, mapped out for any individual, there are from time to time crossroads where the path divides and the person concerned may choose to follow one of two or more futures.

The potential futures would not be radically different from each other but might include interaction with other people. For instance, a person might choose to marry someone or he might choose not to. He might elect to take employment with a certain business house or he might choose another. We wish, therefore, for you to understand that there are these possible branches to your future and it is important for you to make the correct choice, although, strictly speaking, the laws of karma will ensure that you experience the events that you must experience. However, life can be hard or it can be easy. One can blunder along rather like a blind person probing a route that he cannot see or one can view the potential futures and select the one that is most suitable.

Through the process of meditation, prayer, and devotion to God, an aura fills with power that will act to transport you into the akashic area at will. Once you have gained access to that area, you may, as was described above, view past events and learn from them. You may also follow the path of your immediate future and examine where that will take you. As you approach a crossroads, you will see clearly the possible futures that are there. By following in your mind those futures one at a time, you can select one that is most suitable for your development. It is hoped, however, that by the time that you have developed sufficient skill to perform this feat that you will be wise enough to choose a future that will benefit you in the long term and not a future that appears to give you an easy ride through life.

Also, it should be noted that the future is always a little fluid in nature. Although events leading up to a crossroad can be viewed with considerable accuracy and indeed events after a crossroad can be examined and largely relied upon, ultimately, examination proves to be conjecture as more and more variants come into play. That is not to say that the future cannot be manipulated successfully.

Let us imagine that you have examined a series of possible futures and are uncertain as to which one to choose. The course of action is to follow none of them. Sit down and pray to God for guidance. Place yourself in God's hands and allow him to lead you into the future that is the most promising for you. You may also consult with your guides and helpers assuming that you have developed the faculty of clairaudience (telepathy). You will find that God will lead you into the future and you will not go wrong.

It may be noted that many people who have no ability to enter the akashic and have probably never heard of it also place themselves in God's hands and allow Him to lead them into the future. The difference is one of maturity. When you were a child, you allowed your parents to guide you along a street, trusting that you would arrive safely at your destination. Now that you are an adult, you follow your own path and ask for help and guidance only when you are lost. The spiritual path is essentially one of growing up. We encourage you to stop acting like a child and begin to act as a mature adult. We give you eyes to see with, ears to hear, and we give you knowledge of the path that you must take. Then we set you free to walk that path in God and in mature fashion.

You cannot make wise decisions without intelligence and knowledge. Few people indeed who have trod the spiritual path have had the knowledge that we make available to you. We cannot give you intelligence but we have shown you how to develop it. We cannot give you wisdom but, once again, we have shown you how to develop that gift. You are now fully armed to tread the path. You are able to rise in maturity, rise in intelligence, and in wisdom. With those attributes, you may open the door to your future and choose where you want to go. God is everywhere. At the end of each road, he is there. Whether you choose the highway to God or a byway is your decision.

Remember that you are not alone. Remember always that you are part of a group, a team, and that team is also on the path to God and cannot arrive at its destination until you arrive. Therefore, enjoy the scenery en route but do not linger too long enjoying it. You might be delaying the group and that would be impolite. On the other hand, no one expects unseemly haste. God created the world and all that is. It is a thing of beauty and should be examined and admired. The beauty of the world will enlarge the outlook that you have and will bring you joy. Those of you who rush straight into the arms of God have their reward but they miss much of the beauty and wonder of God's kingdom.

Choose the path that you wish to follow and follow it in peace, in love, and in the sureness that you will arrive at your destination. You will meet with us en route. We wait to greet you. We lift you up and carry you with us. Be at one with us. Be at one with all mankind and with all life. Be at one with God. In the name of the Almighty, we seal you and send you on wings of spirit.

Amen.

# CHAPTER 14 - QUESTIONS & ANSWERS

This last chapter will be a bit of an odd sock drawer chapter in which I place the bits and pieces of information that I have added myself after the reading of the actual book. It will be in three parts. The first part explains some of the hidden messages contained in the Bible, the second part will be some meditations given to me by The White Brotherhood, and the last part is a series of questions and answers.

If you have read the book The Stairway Of Freedom up to this point, you will have no doubt realised the truth, spiritual truth, is often very different to the apparent reality that we see and experience in our everyday lives. Well, the same applies to understanding the stories contained in the Bible.

Most Biblical scholars tend to interpret the information as an historical record of certain events that occurred in the Middle East many years ago. In other words, they see the Bible as a history book. According to the information that I have received from The White Brotherhood, this is not at all the case. The Bible is a spiritual textbook concerning you and me and our personal relation to God. If the characters and events that are cited in the Bible actually are historical in nature, that is because the people who wrote the Bible cleverly encoded the spiritual message to conceal the truth from people of less than good intent that might have tried to distort the message hidden in the text.

As the Biblical scholars, priests, etcetera, were not always the most spiritually advanced people in the world, some of them did, and still do, actually worship the dark forces, unbelievable as this seems. Fortunately, the way that the minds of these people work seems to mask them from the true message hidden in the text of the Biblical stories. Other people, of good intent but of limited knowledge, accept the historical content of the stories without question. Studying the historical content will, however, bring little enlightenment but at least these people do no harm either to themselves or to the true seekers after truth.

By way of example to explain in the hidden messages, I would like to quote two of the stories in the Bible and explain the spiritual message behind these two stories. The first story concerns the birth of Christ. The tale, as written in the Bible, states basically that a baby, Christ, was born of a virgin, Mary, in a stable. Now this may or may not be historical fact because, actually, the spiritual message hidden in the story quite simply means this. When a baby is mentioned in the Bible, it always represents your personal aspect of God. A virgin represents your soul and a building of some sort, in this case a stable, represents your physical body. Thus, the story of the birth of Christ quite simply means that you have a personal spirit of God and that spirit is contained in a soul, which is just a protective coating round the spirit of God rather like the shell of an egg protects the embryo bird within, and both the spirit of God and the soul are in association with your body. That's it. That's all the story means.

Now, the second story that I would like to consider is that of David and Goliath. Simplifying the story, it basically states that two armies oppose each other on a battlefield, the Philistines and the Israelites. The Israelites are the goodies and the Philistines are the baddies. However, the Philistines have a giant on their side called Goliath and he is terrifying the Israelites. So the King of Israel asks a shepherd boy named David to sort the problem out. David returns to the battlefront, puts a stone in his sling and throws it at Goliath. The stone finds a chink in Goliath's armour and kills him. The Philistines then run away and the Israelites are victorious.

Now, what this story actually means is that the Philistines are the people around us today that try and destroy our peace and happiness in order to bring profit to themselves. These people would include some politicians, some bankers, some world leaders, and so on. Goliath is quite simply the embodiment of all those bad vibrations. The Israelites represent ordinary good-hearted people, not only Jewish but all people of all race and colour that try to live in peace and harmony with themselves and their neighbours. The Philistines, being at home in an earthly environment, find it quite easy to control and dominate the simple, good souls, bringing mayhem into the lives of millions of us as they put their evil projects into action.

In this story, the King of the Israelites, represented by somebody called Saul, is actually God, the God of all good people. David represents you and me, assuming that we are all good people. So, David, in the story, speaks to King Saul. This means that you and I meditate and connect with God. Through meditation and prayer, we are given an arm, the power of God. The stone that David projects towards Goliath implies that we can pray for our enemies and, through that act, we can direct the mighty force for good, which is God, towards those who would harm us thus rendering evil people powerless to harm us. So, Goliath is slain and the Philistines rendered powerless. The story of David and Goliath quite simply means that, through our connection with God, we are able, by the act of prayer, meditation, and service to our fellow man to render powerless those evil people who would harm us. Believe me. It works. Through prayer, meditation, and by trying to live a life in which we try not to harm people, a barrier surrounds us that evil people cannot penetrate.

There is also another aspect to this act. If we have this barrier protecting us and someone tries to harm us, the evil force that they project towards us bounces off us and returns to them, bringing into their lives the mayhem that they hoped to bring into our lives. It is the nature of evil thought that once sent out by someone it has to find a home before it can stop. If you accept, either willingly or because you do not have a barrier in place, that evil thought, it stops with you. If it bounces off of your shield, it has to return to the sender. However, do not try to send an evil thought back to someone yourself. It does not work like that. Just pray for those who would harm you and the evil force will rebound on its own. You do not have to do anything. Just surround the person trying to harm you with love. Project an emotion of love towards that person or organisation that is trying to harm you and God does the rest. That is the stone that David projected at Goliath.

Thus, I have explained two stories from the Bible and, I hope, demonstrated that the stories relate to you in your everyday lives. Virtually all the tales recounted in the Bible can be decoded in a similar fashion. The same message is repeated again and again. God exists and you are part of that God-force. Of course, you are free to accept or not that which I have explained above. If you wish to visualise God as an old man with a white beard and think of the stories in the Bible as just historical fact, that is up to you.

As an addendum to the book, Stairway To Freedom, I have some meditations and questions and answers that were given to me over a period of time and I would like to present them to you. They may be of interest.

We commence with the meditations which were received periodically over a number of years and were found to be highly beneficial when spoken silently during meditation. The thought pictures summoned by the phrases were instrumental in bringing peace and tranquility during the early stages of a meditation and enabled access to the deep quietness of the mind to be gained with great success. It is hoped that the listener, too, may similarly benefit.

The first meditation was given to me on the 9th of June 1980 by a gentleman called Father Ignatius who, when he was alive on Earth here, was a Benedictine monk, I believe, and he lived in a strangely named abbey in Devon called Blackthorn Abbey. I begin.

If a wheel is considered, say, a heavy cart wheel, the wheel rotates, the rim is heavy, and, so, the wheel turns slowly but powerfully. Imagine that the wheel is life going slowly on and on. You are sitting on the edge of that wheel. All sorts of things are trying to stop the wheel from turning but nothing can. The weight of spirit keeps the wheel turning. Eventually, the wheel completes a revolution and we arrive back at the point that we started at. So, we have achieved nothing. This is not true. Work has been done by the movement of the wheel. Goods have been moved or a pulley has been raised. So it is with life. The movement of the wheel is irresistible. We must go along with it. When the wheel returns to the point from which it started, the measure of achievement is the work done and the service rendered.

A second meditation. I begin.

Let us sit on a beach by the sea. It is a warm sunny day. The sea is calm and the sand hot. As we sit, we pick up a handful of sand and look at it. We see that it is not yellow and smooth. It consists of tiny crystal of many colours. Some of them sparkle like diamonds. We look at the surface of the sand and we realise that at one time long ago this was perhaps a cliff and it has been eroded by the action of waves. Look at the sea – a vast expanse of blue-green water slowly undulating in the gentle breeze. Can we imagine or calculate the quantity of water? Can we see the myriad fishes, plants, animals, and organisms that live beneath the surface? Yet, we know that they exist.

We do not doubt the sky so blue and yet invisible to our eyes. We observe a few birds flying but we cannot see the insects, butterflies, and tiny creatures nor can we see the air currents constantly moving. We accept that they are there. Now the sun – without which nothing can live, the glorious light of warmth that sustains our existence, and yet who can see a sunbeam, who can hold one in his hand? But we do not doubt the power of the sun. Its magnetic pull holds our universe in balance. The waves of the sea are influenced by the magnetic waves of the moon which, once again, are invisible to our senses and yet we know that they are there. So it is with the spirit world. All of it is invisible to our normal senses and yet we can believe that it exists.

We are the lucky ones because we are the chosen people. We who can accept more than our five senses tell us and who believe in the infinite power and creation of God are his chosen people. He sends his angels to guard us and keep us in all our ways. This wonder is sent to us for a simple act of faith because we accept, without question, without doubt, that there is more to our existence than the physical body that we see and that behind everything is our Creator, our Father, Infinite Spirit.

Third meditation. I begin.

Sitting by the side of a stream on a sunny day, watch the water as it bubbles happily along down the mountain. The stream is sheltered by the leaves of trees, giving the water the appearance of myriad, multifaceted diamonds. If we consider one single drop of that water, we are aware of how totally unconcerned it is over its past or its future. It may have spent long years hidden deep in the mountains. It may have had to work its way across miles of stinking marshland. It may have been drunk and eliminated by some animal but all that is behind it. At the moment, it is clean and fresh, full of life and happiness, bubbling along in the sun. It knows not of its future. Round the corner may be a waterfall waiting to dash it against rocks. There maybe a huge lake to absorb it into its stillness, like a form of death. There may be an animal waiting to drink it again. It knows not and it cares not. It was made by God, is from God and it is doing God's will at the moment.

We are slightly different. We have the power to think, to reason, to intellectualise and to fear. We have knowledge of our past which causes us unhappiness if it was bad and unhappiness if it was better than the present. We have awareness that there is a future. We are constantly apprehensive over what the future might bring. This condition may be likened to a drop of water that is trapped in a stinking marsh. It is surrounded by unpleasantness. It has slowly to make its way to the running water again and this may take many, many years. Eventually, it will do so. God wants us to be like the water of a stream. His will is to allow us to be free, to be happy in the moment. We create the marsh with our thoughts and fears. We can, if we wish, turn away from the regrets of the past. They no longer exist, only in our minds. We do not know what lies ahead. Only God knows and his will is that we should have faith in Him like a drop of water. He will deliver us safely through whatever tribulations await us.

The key to getting from the marsh into the clear water of God is prayer and faith. We should pray for guidance, strength, and courage, and in the same breath, thank God for that help that is already available even before we ask. Of course, the future is important and we should be forever open to a change in direction but we should follow God's lead. We cannot force things to happen by our will. By being happy in the moment, we are doing God's will and God will surely look after us. His whole hierarchy of spirit power is sent to strengthen and protect His own and His own are those who trust in and do the will of God.

The next meditation.

Let us walk into a garden, a walled garden, the type that was built into the spacious grounds of large houses many years ago. It is beautifully and tastefully laid out with many roses and flowers of a variety of hues. All are in bloom. Colour is everywhere. The perfume is delightful. Outside the walled garden is an expanse of lawn. Despite the sun overhead, a cold wind blows. The few plants that there are are stunted and unhappy-looking. They have been cut back by the incessant wind, cold, and driving rain. Inside the walled garden, one would imagine oneself to be in a different world. The same sun shines overhead but the high walls keep out the wind and cold. When rain falls, it falls gently and nourishes the plants.

The human condition can be compared to these gardens. Worldly conditions can be harsh and unkind. If we live in the outside world, our development is stunted by the conditions in which we live. We can discover another world, an inner world. Our minds can unlock the door to a world in which the harsh conditions outside cannot affect us. In this inner world, our spirits can flourish and blossom, nourished by the gentle power descending from the spirit world. The door into this inner world can be unlocked by meditation and quiet contemplation.

Another meditation. I begin.

162

Walk with me down an avenue of trees. Note the life that is all around us – the life in those green trees, in the insects, and animals that live in those trees and in the grass underfoot in the Earth. As we take a step along the avenue, imagine each step to represent a day, a week, a season, a year. Between each step, we observe so little change and yet there is great change. All life has developed a little. Some insects and animals have died, some are born, others mature – the same with the plants and trees. All are changed in some way but at the time that we take that one step, we see no change. When we reach the end of the avenue, we look back and we can hardly recognise the avenue as the same one that we started out along. All the trees are different. Most have grown. Some are dead. Others have sprung into life.

And so it is with our human lives. We go through life day by day and observe so little change. It is only when we pause and look back over a period of our lives, or indeed a complete lifetime, that we see much difference. We see how our hopes and ambitions that we started out with have grown to fruition or have withered and died. We see how new hopes have sprung into life. It causes us to wonder as to the nature of the mind that plans the avenue that causes the trees to grow or to die and, if we look closely, we see the mind of God. With our lives, we may also, if we seek, observe the mind of God controlling and engineering everything.

This will be the last meditation and I begin.

Let us walk into a garden and observe the plants growing there. In the middle of the garden is a large tree. This tree has been there for many years since it was planted. One wonders how many summers and winters it has seen, how many droughts and floods, how many birds have nested in its branches, the changes that have been made to the gardens. But the tree is oblivious to it all. It senses the changes in the seasons and it senses drought or flood. However, no matter what occurs and no matter what it senses, its attention never strays from its purpose, its reason for living. That purpose is to achieve perfection. Inside every atom of its totality is the power of God, for ever driving it towards perfection. The tree knows this and concentrates all its attention on achieving this.

However, the perfect tree is a matter of point of view. A bird's eye view of a perfect tree would be one that would provide shelter, food, and a nesting site. A squirrel's idea would be one containing a hollow and food. A human's ideal would be of a tree of a certain size, colour, hardness of wood, etcetera. The tree can never be perfect from another's point of view. It can only be perfect from its own standpoint. Therefore, it tries only to be perfect within its own limitations.

That is the end of the various meditations.

We now come to a number of questions that were posed over a period of time and the answers were given by various guides.

The first one is talking about the miracle of turning water into wine by the master Jesus and this is the answer. It describes a marriage, an event, where the spirit of God normally contained in the soul is joined to the etheric and physical bodies. Three days was the time it took for such an event to occur. Therefore, Jesus represents the spirit of God, his mother represents the soul, and his disciples represent the etheric and physical bodies. When the time came for the spirit of God to merge with the other bodies, the vibrational rate of blood was raised to incorporate the spirit of God. "Woman, what have I to do with thee" is a way of indicating that the soul and body are separate, not one. "Mine hour is not yet come" means the soul and spirit of God is not yet ready to make the final transition back to God. The governor of the feast is God. So when Jesus changed water into wine, he was imbuing the etheric bodies with his spirit.

The next question was this. Do animals eventually progress towards becoming human and, if not, what is the development path of animals? And this is the answer. All life has its place in God's world and the paths of development are quite separate. The rocks, plants, animals, and humans are developing along separate lines and their development is decided and controlled by different types of archangels. All life has a similar goal, that is, perfection. In humans, the individual souls seek a spiritual perfection before merging into a group soul perfection. Animals, plants, and rocks, although they have a spiritual counterpart, that is, a spirit plane where they go between incarnations, are designed to be on Earth. They are creatures of Earth. Each in his species seeks perfection of that species as a creature perfectly adapted to Earth conditions. They will always remain on Earth. They can never be humans.

However, they are developing and ever-changing. If a species is unable to adapt to changing Earth conditions, the physical bodies die out. Their souls go to a plane of animal consciousness and will slowly dissolve into the power which is used to create and strengthen other animals. Some monkeys resemble humans. However, that is coincidence. All animals have to have some particular features and with the great variety of animals that there are, it is inevitable that one species should resemble humans. However, there is no connection.

The next question. Are the spirits and spirits guides that men can contact separate beings from that of men or are they memories from previous incarnations? And this is the answer. All humans are separate entities in the sense that each are individual. Each individual soul, personality, person is a complete being unto himself. He is able to operate successfully as a human person in the meaning that is generally understood on the Earth plane. Each spirit, or spirit guide in the Heaven spheres, is also an individual entity and has his own thoughts, concepts, feelings, ideas. However, just as the atoms that go to make up, say, a car are separate and complete in themselves but nevertheless are bound to travel where that car travels, so all souls are in groups of souls who travel eternity together and are bound together in what may be

164

called a group soul. It is the destiny of that group soul to share problems, assist and advise each other, and to advance as a group towards perfection.

This is all a part of the law of like attracting like. Souls that were conceived at about the same time tend to be at the same state of advancement together and so by the law are attracted to each other. Of course, any individual may advance or slow down as an individual and therefore drop from that group, ultimately to join another group of the same level as himself. Souls at a standstill are attracted to each other. Souls bent on doing evil work are attracted to each other. The group soul to which we, your friends in spirit, both known and unknown, you, your wife, family, and many of your friends with similar interests to yourself belong, have been travelling for many many years. We have seen much, done much, and made many mistakes. Mistakes and triumphs of individuals are felt keenly by the group. In a very real sense, the group soul exists as a single entity and, in that sense, we are all one.

At all times, we are all very close to each other and are in each other's thoughts. Our auras intermingle. If you had the eyes of spirit, you would see the individual auras of the members of the group and also the group aura that results from the intermingling of all the auras. It is not natural for God's creatures to live singly. All of creation operates according to the law of mutual attraction and, ultimately, all the different individuals will merge completely with their group souls and all the group souls will merge into one. That merging happens now and has happened for a long time to more advanced groups. That act, oneness, after merging causes oblivion to the individual and the power released is, of course, the power of God from whence all started.

Another question. What does "forgive yourself first, then forgive others" mean? And the answer comes up now. When we have offended against another, it is not the individual that we have attempted to harm but God made manifest in that man. God would never take revenge against us. His love is total. Therefore, we realise that we have made the cardinal error of offending against someone whom it is impossible to hate because God is total love. We also realise that we are part of God. In offending against another, we are attempting to hurt a brother and our Father. We also are made in God's image. We also have a spark of God in us. It follows that when we attempt to hurt another, we must be attempting to hurt the same God that is present in both parties. We are, therefore, attempting to hurt ourselves. Such a foolish act of harming ourselves can only be pardoned by ourselves. Once we realise this fact and are sorry that we were foolish enough to harm ourselves by attempting to harm another, we are in a position to observe the actions of those who would harm us and forgive them for they know not what they are doing.

Another question. What is God? How did God come about? What was before God? This is actually a four-part answer. The first part. God is the force that we see all around us from which everything is made. We cannot see God, we can only see the effect and know that God is the originator. Second part. God is the natural result of the most fundamental law of the cosmos, the law of mutual attraction. Like attracts like. Before there was any order in the universe, this law was working, attracting molecules of matter together and conversely making space attract space. As atoms come together, this law continues to operate, ensuring that substances of beauty attract other substances of beauty. Discordant shapes attract discordant shapes. Molecules with a tendency towards animate life attract similar elements and so it goes on. Over eons of time, all that we see has been formed by this law. This is the shaping hand of God.

From this spiritual law, beings have similarly developed and other aspects were developed which have resulted in all that we see and know. Now it is so complex that we are able to talk of God as a being but God is the ever-developing result of natural law. God is good because, by the natural law, goodness is more powerful than evil, unity more powerful than chaos. If chaos ruled, there would only be a splitting up until nothing existed, which would be self-defeating. As so much exists, we must accept that goodness is more powerful, therefore, God is goodness. The angels are aware of this and actively work to increase the power of goodness which is God. The Christ called God his father quite rightly because the law of mutual attraction which resulted in substance of a spiritual nature coming together to form the power of goodness was able to cause good matter to mass together which is the intelligence that we know as Christ. This applies equally to us all. There are many other laws that enable the spirit and physical world to operate but this explanation provides a basis for understanding.

The third part. Before God, there was only chaos. Order had not come to the universe because the law of attraction is such that the more spread out the molecules of substance, the more slowly they come together. The statement in the Bible concerning the amount of time God took to form the world can only be taken figuratively.

Rider: We should all believe in God, live a life of godliness, and do God's work because, by doing so, we will bring more and more power of goodness together which will result in ever greater power of God. Any evil thought or action has a result of negating the power of good which is God. If evil, which is chaos, were practiced on a wide scale, destruction of all matter would result. Nothing positive can ultimately be achieved by thinking or doing any action that is negative. Can a house be built by separating and spreading out the bricks and timbers?

Okay. Next question. Animals have illnesses similar to humans. In humans, this is considered to be karmic debt. How can animals incur a debt? And the answer is, animals do not incur a debt as do humans. The illnesses to which animals are subject are there so that the species of animal may develop to perfection. Illnesses sort out the weaker of any species, leaving the stronger animals to carry on. Thus, in nature, all physical life is adapting and evolving towards perfection.

Question. Why is it necessary for us to go through physical life? Have the archangels ever been through similar experiences? Why cannot we choose to be perfect as we were made? And the answer is, when life is created, it is perfect but without experience. Some souls do not need to sense temptation. They know within themselves that they are of God and it is only God-like sentiments that matter. There is no purpose in such souls incarnating on Earth. Experience is gained in the heavenly spheres – experience of helping, of service, of humility, etcetera. They progress towards a state of near perfection and we call them archangels. When they no longer require to be of service, they take a final step and merge into oneness with God.

All souls may progress in a similar fashion at any time. It is not necessary to incarnate again and again. By rejecting temptation and keeping one's whole aim concentrated upon seeking God, a state can rapidly be reached where incarnation is no longer necessary. Then progress can be made through the spiritual spheres. Remember that knowledge does not have to be gained by firsthand experience. By believing in God and by actively seeking the path to perfection, knowledge and power is given by a spiritual process that results in a person knowing what to do and what not to do. By such a process do humble disciples rise to be archangels.

Question. It is stated in the Bible that Jesus said to the rich man in answer to the question as to what he should do to enter the kingdom of Heaven, "sell all you have, give it to the poor, and follow me." In view of that, is it correct for spiritual leaders to live in palaces and to be surrounded by great opulence? And the answer. A person who is spiritually advanced would happily serve God by working and living in whatever circumstances he was required so to do. However, do you think that Jesus lives in squalor? He lives in a great palace, surrounded by things of beauty. This is the inevitable result of the beauty that he exudes from his perfect personality.

In a similar fashion, it is almost inevitable that a true disciple of God, who had made sufficient progress along the path towards God, would attract round him things of beauty. This would include not only buildings and furniture but would indicate that the people with whom he mixed would exude beauty also. This does not imply that the God-filled person is in any way decadent or at fault. It implies that God has rewarded his faithful servant by surrounding him with things of beauty which are his just rewards for service rendered unto God.

Question. For most people, there never seems to be sufficient time in a day to do the things that we have to do and the things that we want to do and yet some people achieve so much in their lifetime. How is this? And the answer. There is always time to do that which we have to do. God always grants us sufficient time, if necessary, through one or more incarnations. Therefore, we should not ever need to hurry. However, life proceeds at its inevitable pace and we often appear like mice in a wheel, racing to keep pace with it. That is because we do not have our lives under control. It is essential to reach into the hidden depths in order to release power that will regulate the pace of our lives until it is in step with the pace of the flow of total life. Then, the two being in phase with each other, difference will disappear and time will appear to be motionless.

If time remains at rest, one has an infinite time in which to achieve that which needs to be accomplished. The means of keeping our lives under control is to locate and tap the hidden spring of spiritual power in the soul. This can be done by meditation and contemplation. Eventually, a stage is reached where one moves in harmony with the flow of life. This can be achieved on Earth during an Earthly incarnation. The result would be a release of sufficient energy to carry out the task in hand, a sense of well-being and of purpose and satisfaction that every task taken will be completed.

Yet another question. On the subject of diet, it is stated that humans travel along one of twelve rays, the signs of the zodiac, but that plants, etcetera, are grouped together according to their species and each species travels along any particular ray. Why is this? The answer. The technique whereby humans incarnate is more complex than the effect that causes vegetables to grow. Humans originate from the same source as does all life, but once the decision is made to direct it in any particular direction, then the routes that are taken, which finish with togetherness on Earth, are different. In the case of a human, the matter is further complicated by the fact that humans are capable of emotions and thoughts, feelings and sensibilities, totally outside of the spectrum that any vegetable would consider. Therefore, it has proved necessary and indeed vital in the final analysis to divide human life into one of the twelve carrier waves and each person created from life force will travel that wave. Vegetables, being much more simple, do not need to be split individually and, therefore, may be grouped and those groups will travel a particular ray.

Further, it will be noted that humans incarnate from one of twelve staging posts according to the time of year that corresponds to the planet Earth becoming in line with any particular one of the twelve holding planets. Vegetables of any particular group come direct from the Earth in that they do not originate in the manner that humans do. If we take the example of a carrot, the new generation of carrots form from the seed heads of the parent carrot. Therefore, the potential, or embryo, carrot is already there. It merely requires for the life force to blend direct from the spiritual realms into the seed of the embryo carrot whereas a human incarnates from a staging post placed between the spiritual realm of creation and the Earth.

Thus, it is possible for all carrots to vibrate to a particular ray, the ray incidentally bearing little relation to time in the accepted sense that humans incarnate. Matter can be conveyed along a carrier wave at will regardless of any time of the year, and this answer also goes on to give some advice which I'll read. Herbs should not be eaten simply to flavour food. They are beneficial to mankind as medicines and, if frequently consumed as part of daily diet, their effectiveness will diminish as the body becomes used to their properties. If it is considered that diet may be bland and that dishes prepared using only the vegetables recommended for an individual of any particular birth sign might be uninteresting, it should be noted that a) the cook should be prepared to experiment with combinations of vegetables, fruits, nuts, and pulses to create dishes of interest, b) diet should be considered to be an act of devotion to God and the limitations compared to a previous diet excepted, c) if the end justifies the means, then the results of following a diet will be radiant health and the sure knowledge that one is following the path that one should.

Printed in Great Britain
by Amazon

25495227R00097